AF843510

NEIGHBOURHOOD CARE AND OLD PEOPLE

Neighbourhood care and old people

A community development project

David Cheeseman, John Lansley and Judy Wilson

Published for
The Nottingham Council of Social Service
by
THE BEDFORD SQUARE PRESS
of the National Council of Social Service
26 Bedford Square London WC1

SBN 7199 0832 9

Printed in England by Latimer Trend & Co Ltd, Plymouth

Contents

Preface

In 1964 a number of attempts to help old people were initiated at neighbourhood level in Nottingham, and were thought by the Nottingham Council of Social Service to merit the support of a full-time worker. The National Corporation for the Care of Old People generously provided funds for the employment of a worker over five years, during which period the two original care groups expanded to fourteen, covering the greater part of the city. The report which follows is an account of this work. Part I gives some of the background to the project, Part II describes the project itself and the worker's role within it, and Part III discusses some of the wider theoretical issues raised.

Such a report inevitably involves summarising material, and in so doing there is a danger of losing sight of the variety of groups who made up the total exercise; accordingly, we have included statistical material relating to individual groups in Appendix 2, for those who wish to study the material more closely.

This report has been written by three people, all of whom were at some time employed in the project which is described. Although only one of the authors is still directly concerned with the work, what follows is inevitably a rather subjective account; on the other hand we hope that there may be some value in publishing a description of a community work project by those who were actually involved in it.

When the project started, community development was a small and esoteric practice. Within the last six years, stimulated by the Seebohm report, there has been a much greater recognition of the potentialities of community work techniques for social welfare agencies, and we hope that this report will be of some help to those engaged in this field, both in old people's welfare committees and in local authority social services departments, and perhaps in wider fields as well.

Naturally, in the course of five years this project has been assisted by a great many people, and it would be invidious to single out any of them by name: our gratitude to them is still very real. We must, however, express our thanks to The National Corporation for the Care of Old People for their continuing support, both financially and by advice and encouragement, throughout the project, and for their further assistance to us with a grant towards the publication of this report. We hope they feel it has been worthwhile.

Following the termination of the grant from The National Corporation for the Care of Old People the council of social service was faced with the decision either to produce its report on the five years' work and then sever links with the movement, or somehow to incorporate the work with the duties of existing staff. It was agreed that the work should continue to be supported by the council of social service whilst the local authority social services department was developing its structure and policy in the hope that the department would undertake a commitment of their resources to this work, either through the council of social service or directly from the department. The council of social service staff involved at neighbourhood level in the course of their work are the general secretary, the assistant secretary, the old people's welfare committee secretary, the young volunteer worker and the training officer. These workers have each accepted responsibility for neighbourhood work in a geographical sector of the city—sectors which are coterminous with the social services department boundaries for area teams—and deal with all neighbourhood community issues for their sector whilst continuing to operate on a city-wide basis with their other more specialist work. This is proving particularly useful in facilitating co-operation between the social services department area teams and the voluntary movement at neighbourhood level.

DAVID CHEESEMAN
JOHN LANSLEY
JUDY WILSON

Nottingham 1971

Abbreviations

Abbreviations often supply an unnecessary mystical cloak for social workers, but there are some occasions when they can save repetition; we give below those which have been used in this report.

DHSS	Department of Health and Social Security; formerly
MSS	Ministry of Social Security
NCCOP	National Corporation for the Care of Old People
(N)CSS	(Nottingham) Council of Social Service
(N)OPWC	(Nottingham) Old People's Welfare Committee
WRVS	Women's Royal Voluntary Service

CARE GROUPS IN NOTTINGHAM 1970

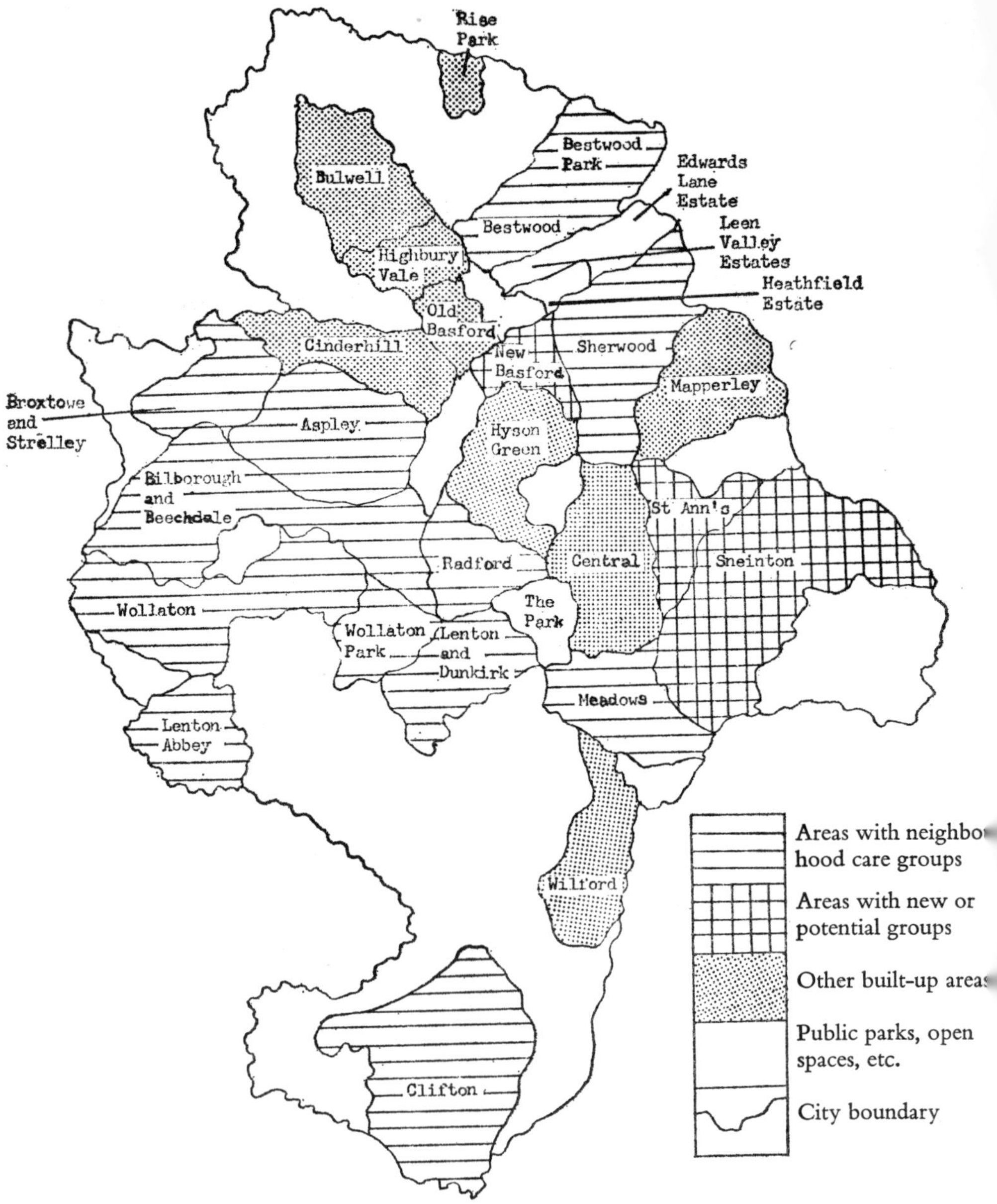

PART I

Background to the Project

CHAPTER 1

Introduction

THE CITY OF NOTTINGHAM

Nottingham is the largest town in the East Midlands, with a population of 305,000. Although it is an old city, with a literary background including D. H. Lawrence as well as Byron, it gives an initial impression of a modern, clean, prosperous town, a centre of light industry (chemicals, tobacco, bicycles, women's clothing), perhaps not very different from many other places. Close examination, however, reveals a more complex pattern. As it has expanded—particularly during the last hundred years—Nottingham has absorbed a variety of pre-existing villages which have retained their identity, while other more recent developments, whether down-town slums, new housing estates or prosperous suburbs, have been quick to take on an identity of their own. A sense of neighbourhood is felt by the inhabitants who will often identify themselves with an easily-recognised part of the city. Thus, although Nottingham has developed in the classic pattern of a series of concentric rings, with decaying working-class housing around the commercial centre and surrounded in its turn by middle-class suburbs and corporation housing estates, this pattern is broken and modified by the existence of cohesive neighbourhoods.

SERVICES FOR THE ELDERLY

In 1966 there were about 45,000 people in Nottingham of pensionable age and over—14·75% of the city's population (corresponding to a national proportion of 15·4%); 11,000 lived alone, 12,300 were over seventy-five. Services for the elderly provided by the local authority in 1966 were almost identical per head of population with the national average in terms of staffing, though below average on expenditure, but the demand for services—especially domiciliary services such as home helps—was often greater than resources available, and at all times staff were fully stretched.

We must add to this, however, services provided by local hospitals, particularly in the field of geriatric mental health. Mapperley Mental Hospital had for a number of years been working to board out their patients in the community, and it was as an extension of this that the medical superintendent, Dr Duncan Macmillan, took much of the initiative in setting up the Sherwood Care Group. Later, Dr Macmillan became chairman of the Nottingham OPWC. In addition to the work at Mapperley there is a special geriatric assessment unit at St Francis' Hospital, where elderly people are accepted for observation, under a scheme run jointly by the hospital and the city and county welfare authorities.

On the voluntary side, there is the usual pattern of services: to mention a few, a number of charities provide accommodation in homes and almshouses, and a charitable dispensary continues to provide a chiropody service. The WRVS covers most of the city with its meals-on-wheels service. These, like other bodies such as the Royal Midland Institute for the Blind and the Salvation Army Social Services Goodwill Centre act as agents for the local authority in providing various kinds of specialist care.

THE NOTTINGHAM COUNCIL OF SOCIAL SERVICE AND OLD PEOPLE'S WELFARE COMMITTEE

The Nottingham Old People's Welfare Committee is a standing committee of the Nottingham Council of Social Service, and it was, to a significant degree, through the interaction of these two bodies that the neighbourhood care schemes arose. Up to the inception of these schemes the OPWC had been involved with the usual old people's welfare activities: it serviced over-sixty clubs, arranged outings, organised a centrally-based visiting scheme, distributed parcels at Christmas, ran a number of old people's homes, and acted as a forum for other agencies involved in these fields. The council of social service, for its part, undertook co-ordinating functions between voluntary organisations, pioneered new developments, and during the early 1960s was becoming increasingly interested and involved in the developing field of neighbourhood work. It was also concerned with the allied field of community (race) relations, and the local community relations council was one of its standing committees.

NATIONAL TRENDS

Mention of community work raises the question of the relation of what was happening in Nottingham to some broader developments at national level. The concept of neighbourhood groups arose in various parts of the country in the early 1960s, and towards the end of the decade was finding expression in a variety of official reports—the Seebohm report on local authority social services (especially Chapter 16), the Skeffington report on public participation in planning, and the Royal Commission on Local Government. Through all these, and in other publications and discussions as well, ran the idea of reconciling the apparent efficiency of the large organisation with the personal needs of the individual consumer, and the consequent need to involve him in the planning stages of the service. At the same time there came a recognition that people in local communities were capable of considerable achievements in determining their needs and taking action to meet them, both through 'self-help' activities and in bringing pressure to bear on other suppliers of services. These two trends have become known as community organisation and community development, and since both these terms are used with a variety of meanings, we have included some definitions in Appendix 1.

Other national trends can also be seen in the Nottingham project. The young volunteer movement, which was also gaining impetus during the early 1960s, found its expression in the appointment of a Community Service Volunteer, with a grant from the King George's Jubilee Trust, to stimulate voluntary service by young people among the elderly. This grant was subsequently applied to the salary of a full-time assistant secretary of the OPWC.

Nor were these trends only apparent within the CSS. It will be seen in the subsequent narrative how in many cases the local churches were instrumental in setting up care groups and this too can be seen as part of a wider movement on the part of churches and clergy to discover new roles for themselves in the local community. The same could be said too of other professions, not least in social work itself; moves to 'community care' in child care and mental health* were also apparent in the field of old people's welfare and books critical of institutional provision such as Peter Townsend's *The Last Refuge* were followed up by the government's ten-year plan for health and welfare services, *Community Care*, published in 1963. Indeed, by the end of the decade the focus of operation had been so widely (if vaguely) accepted that there seemed to be scarcely a service, from the police to the primary school, which was not at risk of having the prefix 'community' slapped on to it, and it is perhaps worth reiterating the warnings given in the early 1960s by writers such as Professor Titmuss that enthusiasm must be followed up by considerable investment in resources, expertise and understanding. Semantics are no substitute for social provision.

CARE GROUPS—THE INITIAL IMPETUS

As we have seen, the council of social service was already interested in various forms of community work, both in the race relations field and, perhaps in a rather unsystematic fashion, in stimulating community develop-

* It could be asked whether the adoption of the term 'community care' in the mental health field as an alternative to institutional care may have distracted attention from wider possibilities of involving ordinary members of the public in caring for people.

ment as and where local initiatives were to be found. It was thus natural when in 1964 groups of people in two areas of the city, The Meadows and Sherwood, became concerned with the needs of their local communities and tried to mobilise local people to meet these needs, that they should have sought the advice and assistance of the council of social service. The CSS was aware of the need to foster these local initiatives, which were otherwise in danger of petering out. At the same time, it was fortunately placed to involve the old people's welfare committee in these developments. The original groups had not turned to the OPWC since it was perceived by them as a traditional welfare-oriented body which seemed to have little relevance to community development. The committee was, however, anxious to be involved in these schemes and saw in them a promising way of fostering and channelling the goodwill and concern for the elderly which was undoubtedly felt by many people in the community. Accordingly, an application was made to NCCOP for a grant to appoint a development officer who would seek to apply the experiences of these areas to other parts of the city—not blindly imposing a uniform pattern but stimulating local initiatives which without such support might have proved abortive. The application was successful, and the development officer* took up his post in October 1965 with the following terms of reference.

1. To carry out a continuing assessment and appraisal of the neighbourhood group concept in the field of old people's welfare, both as a model for Nottingham and perhaps nationally.
2. To carry out a continuing survey and evaluation of the optimum methods for deploying, mobilising, and expanding voluntary services for old people on a neighbourhood basis, taking due account of the differences between areas and the need for flexibility of pattern.
3. To assist in the development of the existing schemes according to their different needs.
4. To promote machinery for co-operation between and co-ordination of the different schemes. At this point, the work of the development officer would be merged with the general work of the old people's welfare committee.

What follows is a record of how this policy worked out during the following five years.

* The first development officer to be appointed had previously been a community worker with Swindon Corporation; when he became secretary of the Nottingham Council of Social Service in 1970 he was succeeded by a former staff member of the National Council of Social Service Community Work Division.

PART II

The Development of Neighbourhood Care Groups

CHAPTER 2

Two Care Groups

By the end of the five-year development period there were fourteen neighbourhood care groups in Nottingham. They had developed in different ways from different beginnings; they had improvised a wide variety of organisational structures, and they had all worked towards their own relationship with other groups and institutions, both locally and on a city-wide basis. The main purpose of this report is to draw out the common experiences and lessons which have been learned from this method of working, but in doing so there is a danger of failing to convey what the individual groups were actually like. Accordingly, we start this section by describing the two oldest care groups, which in some ways typify the two main strands of development.

SHERWOOD

To the north, the city centre straggles up Mansfield Road, and finally expires at the traffic lights at the top of the hill. The change from city to suburb is unmistakeable. To the left stretches the Forest recreation ground, enlivened once a year by the Goose Fair. To the right one senses through the trees the opulent heights of Mapperley. And ahead as Mansfield Road starts downhill again, lies Sherwood, the archetypical suburb. There is a long road with clusters of shops increasing in frequency, reaching their climax in the Metropole cinema and flanked on either side with between-wars housing, and further out a council estate and some expensive private developments. It is comfortable, pleasant, unpretentious. About 23,000 people live in Sherwood, and about 3,000 are of pensionable age, often the original owner-occupants: perhaps a quarter of them live on their own.

In 1964 the geriatric liaison discussion group of Mapperly Mental Hospital approached the Sherwood Community Association to ask whether they would undertake a long-term experiment in the community care of elderly people. The community association was approached because at this time it was pursuing a particularly outward-going policy and its community service committee had already been active in forming a play-group and a club which provided limited employment for elderly people. It also had the advantage of an active, full-time warden.

The local council of churches and the city welfare services department were also brought into the discussions, and the outcome was the creation of the Sherwood Community Care Group, with four objectives:

(i) drawing up a list of elderly people in the neighbourhood;
(ii) establishing a panel of visitors, and a suitable training programme for them;
(iii) creating a combined lunch club and day centre;
(iv) liaising between local voluntary effort and those working professionally in the health and welfare field.

These objectives have remained fairly constant, and have met with considerable success.

Contact

Records of elderly people in the area were built up rapidly. Within a few months some 700 names were listed, and since then, there has been a continuing effort to find people in need of help. The idea of a survey of the whole area was rejected because it was felt that the group might not be able to deal with all the needs which might be uncovered; however, there have been surveys of smaller areas carried out by the local churches from time to time, and in addition clergy supply lists of people who have recently been bereaved, enabling them to be contacted to discover whether they need any help. Pre-paid postcards are left with elderly people enabling them to ask for help more easily.

The committee is in touch with some 450 elderly people at Christmas (when parcels and cards are distributed) and gives some help throughout the year to over half of these.

Visiting

As regards visiting, by 1970 there were about sixty volunteers each regularly visiting one or two old people. An initial training course for visitors was not well attended, and regular visitors' meetings, planned to be held every eight weeks, ended up as annual events. However, the appointment of a voluntary visiting organiser in 1970 seems to have improved the situation: she regularly meets visitors individually to discuss problems which they may have, and contact is also maintained through a newsletter.

Lunch club

The lunch club was the first major activity of the group. Starting at the community centre in December 1964 twice a week for ten people, it has now expanded to four days a week for twenty-five people each day. Meals are supplied by a local hospital and the club is staffed by volunteers. Transport is also provided by volunteers, including some of the mothers of children who attend the pre-school playgroup held at the centre.

The success of the lunch club, however, brought with it problems, particularly the amount of time involved for the group's secretary. Consequently, a part-time paid organiser was appointed in 1967, and a separate lunch club sub-committee of the community centre was established.

Liaison and co-operation

Liaison between volunteers and professionals is maintained at a formal level through bi-monthly meetings of the committee. This meets in the afternoon for the convenience of professional workers and the membership covers a wide range of organisations and individuals concerned with the elderly. Discussions often cover general issues as well as the organisation of services, and the meetings have proved to be a very useful forum.

One characteristic of the group has been that it has tended to limit its attention quite specifically to the elderly, seeing itself as an old people's welfare organisation rather than as a general focus for community needs or action. This has perhaps been unfortunate, since there has subsequently been a change at the community centre, and the community service committee, which might have helped people with other kinds of problems, has fallen into abeyance. On the other hand, this approach has obvious strengths in concentrating resources into a particular area.

There may be a widening of the group's activities in the future. One of the small surveys of old people's needs mentioned earlier revealed incidentally that many young wives in Sherwood were in need of support. Partly at the instigation of the ex-development officer, it was decided in 1970 to establish a working party to examine ways in which the group ought to expand its work to help mothers and children.

Clearly the administrative and financial requirements of a scheme of this nature are substantial. The lunch club was started with a £400 grant from a local charitable trust for necessary alteration to the community centre canteen and for the purchase of equipment. The care group now receives an annual grant of £130 from the corporation health and welfare committee, which includes a grant for the running of the lunch club and payment of the organiser. This income is supplemented by local fund-raising efforts and donations: the total budget of the group is £230 p.a.

The chairman of the group is the local vicar (who has subsequently become in addition chairman of the council of social service). The secretary, who was honorary assistant secretary of the community association, is a part-time research worker and is supported in her work by a number of assistants. This delegation of responsibilities has proved vital in view of the extent of the group's activities. The community centre provides a useful focal point and administrative centre—including such important functions as being able to take telephone messages in the secretary's absence.

How far does the Sherwood Community Care for the Elderly Committee* differ from a good old people's welfare committee covering an area of similar size? The emphasis on good co-operation between services working in the area, the recruitment of volunteers, the maintenance of efficient up-to-date records, the high standards of care: these are all activities which an OPWC would undertake—and criteria by which it would be judged. Perhaps the model by which we should assess this work is that of community welfare organisation, the optimum deployment of services, maybe made more efficient because of concentration on a relatively small district. But the very specific title of the Sherwood committee, is perhaps an indication of the limitations of its activities. Old people *in* the community are served very effectively; but what impact does the group have on the community as a whole, or vice versa? Is there a quality of 'Sherwoodness' about the activities of this group which differentiates it from any other old people's welfare service anywhere else? Should we expect there to be? These questions are not criticisms; after all it may well be that the need for self-expression by the wider community is met by the community association, and almost certainly the clear-sighted definition of the committee's objectives have helped it to achieve what it has done. Nor should we forget that its present form was, after all, created by local people. In raising these questions we are trying to bring out some particular qualities of the committee which enable it to serve as one model of what a care group may be like, and to illustrate more strongly the contrasts with the second group.

MEADOWS GROUP

Most people, leaving Nottingham railway station, turn right towards the centre of the town. If you turn left, you find yourself in the Meadows. A flat triangle of land jutting out into a bend of the Trent, it was built over in the 1860s and 1870s: workmen's houses surrounding small factories are bounded on the west by the railway marshalling yards. It still bears the marks of that haphazard development: there are small terraced houses with little back-yards, grouped together in odd squares and triangles and interspersed with corner shops (some now catering for the appreciable immigrant population), pubs,

* Changed its name in 1966.

churches, and more recently, launderettes. Much of the housing is in the state one would expect after a hundred years' weather beating on shoddy building, though this would not be true for all the area. Slum clearance has at last started, with a ten-year programme which will result in the present population of 22,000 people being halved and all but the Trent Bridge area being demolished and rebuilt. There are at present about 3,000 people aged sixty and over in the area.

Although many of the local residents will probably be glad to leave the Meadows many others still retain quite a strong community sense. In either case, they share many of the problems common to such a run-down area: urban decay affects not only individual houses but also the whole physical and social fabric of an area. Typically (the pattern can be found in Sparkbrook, in Toxteth, in Notting Hill) this produced a response from the local social workers who met together to look at the needs of the area under the chairmanship of the local Methodist minister and with the general secretary of the CSS as secretary. Local people were brought in to create a forum which would encourage and support initiatives to meet local needs, and some voluntary workers came from outside the area, perhaps drawn initially by the 'romantic' aspect of a run-down working-class area. But they stayed, too. So, in 1963, the Meadows Group was formed. The group is now regularly supplied with information from the city planning department about the future of the district, and has started its own newspaper, the *Meadows Mail*, to spread this information throughout the area.

The main forum soon created sub-groups to take up specific tasks and the first major project that the group concerned itself with was an experimental play leadership scheme, which was organised in a local park in the summer of 1964. This proved a success, and was subsequently taken over by the corporation parks department and extended to other areas of the city. In the same year, a pre-school playgroup was started with financial support from the Save the Children Fund: it has continued and now meets five mornings a week in the Methodist church hall.

A second area of activity was the amenities committee. This was formed because of local concern about derelict property and the accumulation of rubbish, particularly on deserted sites and in back alleys. Regular 'rubbish drives' were arranged in which volunteers cleared these areas, helped by the loan of a corporation cleansing department lorry. This committee took on a much wider role when an ex-town planner spent about a year in the area as a community worker. Thanks to his enthusiasm and expertise the committee began to take a much wider interest in redevelopment proposals for the area (including representing the interests of local residents affected by compulsory purchase orders at a public enquiry).

The third constituent committee of the Meadows Group, and the one with which we are most closely concerned, is the old people's welfare section. In the spring of 1965 a pilot survey to establish the needs of elderly people showed the inadequacy of the current records of welfare agencies and so the whole area was subsequently surveyed. Needs found through this survey have been met in a variety of ways. A visiting service has been built up on existing groups of church workers, and in addition efforts have been made to utilise the networks of good neighbours that already existed. This has proved important in an area with few volunteers coming in from outside, and where there is little tradition of people formally volunteering to help others. There is, however, a considerable tradition of neighbourliness, and efforts have been made to build on this and on existing family networks whenever possible; this has left the group free to concentrate on the hard core of old people who lack such support—those who have no family, or have alienated their neighbours by their constant demands, or are mentally confused.

The establishment of new lunch clubs and social clubs for old people has shown a similar attempt to maximise the potential resources of the area: thus for example demands for further over-sixty clubs have been met by establishing clubs in the halls of churches which have not previously run them. This has enabled the needs of old people in different parts of the area to be met, and it has also tapped new sources of voluntary helpers. In such ways a deliberate policy has been followed both to ensure an adequate coverage of services throughout the area, and to bring in the help of as many local organisations as possible. A further example of the latter can be seen in the involvement of local schools, which have assisted at lunch clubs and have given practical help such as decorating and shopping to individual old people. One school runs a weekly coffee morning for elderly people living nearby as part of its social studies curriculum.

In addition to supporting and extending existing services, the group has developed new ones, in particular the establishment of a day centre for elderly people who have become isolated through physical handicap or mental frailty; it now runs on two days a week. Such a scheme involved considerable organisation and co-operation: with voluntary workers to help staff the centre, with the church whose (modern) hall is used, with the St John Ambulance Brigade, who originally supplied transport and the city welfare services department who provide meals, with welfare workers and the geriatric unit at St Francis' Hospital, and with suppliers of materials for handicraft work. The day centre has also involved the Meadows Group in considerable expenditure, of the order of £4 a week.

The co-ordinating work of the committee can also be seen in the way in which it took the initiative in convening case conferences, attended by workers from both statutory and voluntary services, to discuss needs of individual old people. Such conferences are common enough in child care and family casework, but they are perhaps less common in the field of old people's welfare, and it says a lot for the status of the Meadows Group that statutory workers were prepared to accept such an initiative coming from a voluntary body. More general contact is maintained through a social workers' lunch club, which regularly draws sixty people together.

Any scheme of this kind weighs heavily on a fairly small number of people, even when, as in the Meadows, responsibility for various pieces of work is spread round local organisations. In addition to the administrative work involved the secretary, who lives outside the area, carried a considerable load of responsibility, even if the need was 'just' for referral to another agency, in handling problems of individual old people, who often required considerable material, social and medical assistance. In addition the lack of an adequate administrative base in the area—the community centre has no full-time staff, though there is a devoted voluntary warden, and had no telephone until 1970—meant that the organisers had to 'farm out' such tasks as typing and duplicating to local schools and other organisations. This assisted the development of the group, although it increased the co-ordinating work of the secretary. In 1969 it was decided to make an application to the NCCOP for a grant to employ a worker on a full-time basis, to co-ordinate voluntary help, promote new schemes and undertake administration. A grant of £1,500 p.a. for two years* was made, and the secretary was appointed to the post.

Administration has largely been based on the local community centre, but in addition it has always been possible to make contact with the group at other contact points, such as through the playgroup at the Methodist church hall.

The Meadows Group has also at various times had the services of a Community Service Volunteer who for six months worked to develop voluntary service by young people in the area, and of a community worker who spent about a year in the area. Both these appointments were made possible by grants from local trust funds. It seems likely that such appointments will be necessary in areas like the Meadows where it is difficult to call on administrative and professional skills, as one could perhaps in a middle-class neighbourhood. However, workers in such a setting, with few of the supports which professional workers can normally rely on, can be subject to very considerable strains and may be stretched to near breaking point by voluntary employers who do not appreciate the stresses of their work.

With the expansion of these activities, the costs of the Meadows Group have

* Later extended to three years.

been considerable, and since the day centre started the group has had to find over £1,000 p.a. In 1969–70 they received a grant of £55 from the city health and welfare committee, and other money has been found through local and city-wide fund-raising activities. To facilitate this and the employment of staff, the group has registered as a charity.

Simply to recount activities in this fashion may not bring out the particular character of the Meadows Group. As far as possible the group has tried to reflect the neighbourhood, both as a resource and as the constituency from which it receives its rationale. As regards old people's welfare, strong efforts have been made to interest and involve local organisations, commercial undertakings (corner shops, etc.) and individuals in sharing the community's responsibility for its elderly members. At the same time the flexibility and general frame of reference of the Meadows Group as a whole have made it possible to consider the total needs of the area without losing the detailed attention necessary for promoting particular schemes. Membership of the group is a mixture of local social workers, teachers and clergy and of local residents.

It is the group's desire to be seen as a channel through which local people can express and activate their wishes for the area, and the steps taken to make this a reality, which enables us to treat the Meadows Group—again, with some over-simplification—as a model of the community development approach. This flexibility was built in by the original founders of the group, social workers and clergy who wanted to create a body which would reflect the changing needs of the neighbourhood and in which local people could be involved and it has almost certainly contributed to the group's success. Indeed it may well be that both Sherwood and the Meadows have succeeded because the form and style of operation has reflected local attitudes which, in their turn, may partly be influenced by the different class structure of the two areas.

In Sherwood, a mainly middle-class area, one could perhaps anticipate that local people would have a clearer grasp of organisational structure, a desire to define objectives, to aim for efficiency (without, of course, implying any diminution in care or concern)—and the outcome of these has been the Sherwood Community Care for the Elderly Committee. In the Meadows people are more easy-going about details of services which are lumped together as 'the Welfare' or 'the Corpy'. The Meadows Group has reflected this in its general approach, less organisational than organic, responding as best it can to the evolving life of the local community. We are not arguing that one approach is better than the other: rather, that they may both, in their own ways, be valid responses to the communities which they serve.

CHAPTER 3

Setting up Care Groups

Although we have used the Meadows and Sherwood Groups as examples of care groups, it must be stressed that in many ways they are not typical—particularly in the length of time they have existed, the size of their operations and in employing full- or part-time staff. Another way in which they are untypical is that they were founded before the appointment of the development officer, and consequently without his initial assistance. (It is not, of course, suggested that this help was essential, and indeed some other groups were later set up without assistance from the NOPWC.)

Insofar as one can speak of a standard pattern, there were usually three stages in the establishment of a care group.

(a) An initial approach from one or more individuals or groups in the area to the development officer, suggesting that a care group might be appropriate or desirable for the neighbourhood.
(b) Exploratory discussions with other appropriate individuals or groups, enquiring into the feasibility of a scheme and enlisting their support.
(c) The holding of an inaugural meeting at which the decision to form a care group was taken, followed by the appointment of officers, and decisions on geographical boundaries and broad policy lines for the group's activities.

This may look straightforward enough at first sight, but a number of comments must be made.

THE FIRST APPROACH FROM THE AREA

The development officer preferred to wait for these approaches, rather than to take the initiative by moving into an area to establish a scheme.* Such a policy implies a respect for people's right to determine the running of their own local affairs, and is based on the assumption that initiatives arising spontaneously from the community are more likely to succeed and last than those

* The original terms of reference provided for this possibility, but the worker was always kept fully occupied with spontaneous initiatives from the neighbourhood.

imposed from outside, since the local people have in consequence a greater commitment to such schemes. It also means that the forms taken by groups are more likely to reflect the needs and potentials of the area than would a standard blue-print.

In practice, things do not work out quite so simply. It is not the community which takes initiatives, but individuals within it, and one may ask how representative they always were of the neighbourhood on whose behalf they took action. Sometimes first approaches arose through discussions between organisations in the area, or the first move might be a letter from an individual in an area who was worried about services for the elderly but did not know what could be done for them. In a few cases the first enquiry came from an old person in need of help. The success of one scheme could interest or inspire another area, which could lead to the dangerous assumption that one scheme could provide a blue-print for another.

Often it is not possible to determine the exact source of a first approach, but Table I attempts some breakdown. It should be noted that in some cases more than one group was involved.

EXPLORATORY DISCUSSIONS

The questions to be determined in these discussions were: (i) the boundaries of the neighbourhood, as most people perceived them; (ii) the needs of old people—and others—within the area; (iii) services available at the present time; (iv) potential sources of further help from local organisations (churches, community associations, schools, etc.); (v) the feasibility of establishing a care group in terms of resources available; (vi) possible activities of the care group. Even this programme is over-simple: questions about needs and resources in the area could lead on to a total examination of the neighbourhood, ranging much wider than specific problems of old people or services for them. The persons who had made the first approach would be encouraged to make these soundings-out himself, but there were occasions when the development officer also became involved in the discussions. These would as far as possible be held with most of the major organisations which it was hoped to involve in the care group, including existing services for the elderly, such as statutory workers and leaders of local over-sixty clubs, clergy, community associations and sometimes schools if they were already involved in community service in the locality. Discussions could be prolonged; some organisations could, and occasionally did, feel that outsiders were trying to take over work which they were already doing themselves, or saw attempts at co-ordination as an exercise in empire-building by the OPWC. Often scepticism was encountered: 'People round here don't help one another' or 'everyone's too heavily committed'.

On the other hand there were also those who welcomed the fact that someone was at last taking the initiative: whatever one may think of the adequacy of services, there is at least a general acceptance in the community of the desirability of helping the elderly, compared with attitudes to some other clients of the social services, such as the mentally ill or discharged prisoners.

TABLE I

Source of first approach or initiative in the establishment of care schemes

Source	*Number of schemes in which initiative taken*
Church	8
School	1
Community association	1
Residents' association	1
Councillor	2
Hospital	1
Over-sixty club	1
Individuals	2
Total number of care schemes	14

Note: For break-down by care groups, see Appendix 2, Table A1.

THE INAUGURAL MEETING*

This was held at some convenient point in the area, and invitations were sent to as many local organisations and individuals thought to be sympathetic to the scheme as could be discovered in the course of the preliminary conversations. Topics discussed at the meeting were usually similar to those which had been talked about with individual organisations previously, and the handling of the meeting often became a matter of a delicate balance between presenting ideas which had arisen from those discussions as *faits accomplis*, and getting bogged down in interminable arguments over where precisely some small stretch of the district boundary ran. It was generally hoped that by the end of the meeting the decision to form a care group would have been taken, and a committee appointed. This was not always possible, however, and sometimes a meeting

* Although a public meeting is described here, and was usually recommended by the development officer to try to avoid excluding anyone who might be interested in the group, there were also groups which started as a result of a smaller meeting, or by setting up a specific project from which they later developed.

would be adjourned for a few weeks to enable further negotiations to take place.

All of this may sound a great deal of effort, but it was necessary if the group was to start with sufficient backing from the local community. This meant going at the community's own pace, and ensuring that everyone was clear both as to what was being proposed, and as to the extent of their own commitment. Without this a care group, which was after all dependent on local people to run it and to provide services, could scarcely have survived.

CHAPTER 4

Care Group Services

NEEDS OF THE ELDERLY

We have been discussing the needs of old people as though the exact nature of these needs could be taken for granted. Within broad limits this may be so, but it is desirable to identify them, if only to indicate the limited areas in which care groups were able to make any direct contribution.

Even to talk about the 'old', of course, begs a great many questions. The needs of a married couple where the husband has just retired at sixty-five are likely to be very different from those of a widow of eighty. In most cases, needs increase with age: even though some problems, such as reduced income, may start on the day a man reaches his sixty-fifth birthday, he may still be able to modify its effects through part-time earnings during the first ten years or so of his retirement.

In the section that follows, we discuss the needs and problems of the elderly under four headings: financial, environmental, medical and social.

Financial

Although important and relatively immediate, loss of wages is only one of the problems to be faced. Private pensions and savings may be eroded by inflation, and although pensions have increased more or less proportionately with the general standard of living, the level of payment is still low. Although old people may not be as conscious of their relative deprivation as are some other low-income groups, the effects are still apparent: inadequate nutrition and heating, with implications for physical and mental well-being, limitations on mobility and outside interests which may affect a person's social life, and problems associated with a poor environment.

Environmental

Environmental factors are likely to be important for old people. Like housewives with small children, they will probably spend the greater part of their time in quite a small geographical area, and changes in that environment will thus be of considerable significance to them. This is of particular importance to those who live in decaying down-town areas or who are moved, because of slum clearance, to new estates away from family, friends and familiar landmarks. The maintenance of their homes may also become more difficult, because of lack of financial resources and a diminished ability to do decorating, repairs or gardening themselves.

Medical

A further factor which must be borne in mind is that more people are surviving to an advanced age, thanks to modern medical techniques. This means, however, that they become more dependent on medical care as they grow older, and this again carries implications both for caring for old people when they are ill, and for keeping an eye on those 'at risk'. We need a wider concept of medical care than just the professional treatment of illness, which will include the total needs of the patient for 'care' as well as 'cure'.

Social

Although most recent surveys have stressed that the majority of old people with children see them frequently and receive help from them, there are still many who do not have support from children or near relatives and so are particularly vulnerable when some of the problems we have described earlier arise.

Other social contacts are therefore important. Some of these come with retirement, and needs, for alternative activities and comradeship, to those of work. Over time elderly people's social contacts will probably lessen: friends die, and they themselves become less mobile, particularly if their health deteriorates, until a vicious circle of physical deterioration, social isolation and mental confusion can set in if people become housebound: as we have seen, the Meadows day centre was planned to help people of this kind. Clearly, taking a wider view, it is in this social field that care groups are capable of making their major direct contribution. They cannot provide professional medical services, better housing or higher pensions—any more than can most other welfare agencies: at best they can bring pressure to bear on those who do control these things.

Some of the needs of old people which care groups felt capable of meeting will be examined later when we discuss activities, but we have some limited information about needs, as seen by those who contacted care groups to request their help (see Table 2). Most of these referrals came from statutory or voluntary agencies but nearly a tenth came from old people themselves.

These figures require some explanation. In 1969 three care groups—the

TABLE 2

Reasons for first referrals of old people to three care groups, 1969

Nature of referral (1)	*Clifton*	*Meadows*	*Sherwood*	*Total*
(a) *Medical*				
Injury, illness, etc.	5	14	3	22
Hospital discharge		1	1	2
Mental confusion		21	1	22
Chiropody		1		1
Holiday	1			1
Transport			2	2
Rehousing	2	6		8
Total	8	43	7	58
(b) *Domestic*				
Decorating and repairs	2	12		14
Gardening	3	1		4
Shopping	2	1		3
Domestic chores (cooking, cleaning, etc.)	3	1	2	6
Meals-on-wheels	11 (2)			11
Home help		2	1	3
Total	21	17	3	41
(c) *Social*				
Loneliness, visitor	8	7	6	21
Sitting in, day care		9	3	12
Lunch club			1	1
Christmas parcel or card (3)	2	1	38	41
Total	10	17	48	75
(d) *Miscellaneous*				
Financial difficulties, clothing		4		4
Recently bereaved		1	2 (4)	3
Care group asked to assess new case		4	2	6
Query over service being received		3		3
Total	—	12	4	16
TOTAL	39	89	62	190

Notes:

1 In some cases more than one reason for referral may have been given for the same old person.

2 Clifton, the only area in the city not covered by the WRVS meals-on-wheels service, runs its own scheme.

3 Differences in methods of recording make it impossible to compare the Sherwood figures with those for the other two groups on this item.

4 This figure does not include referrals passed on to Sherwood group by clergy who have officiated at funerals.

Meadows, Sherwood and Clifton (a large new corporation estate on the edge of the city) were asked to keep records of cases referred to them during that year. Records were not always kept accurately, and were in any event limited to new cases rather than those already known to the group, so these figures cannot be seen as a total picture of care groups' work. Nevertheless, they may help to give some picture of the kind of needs which care groups were called on to meet.

Some of the variations in these figures can be explained by the nature of the area: the Meadows, for example, with a high proportion of poor housing, receive many more requests for help with decorating and repairs. Here, too, a deliberate policy of creating links with medical social workers is shown in the number of hospital discharge referrals.

It would be dangerous to carry the interpretation beyond this. The figures are not so much a reflection of the needs of the elderly as of referring agencies' knowledge of the groups' existence, and expectations of what help the groups could provide. The exact nature of the help which groups actually gave will be discussed in the next section.

IDENTIFYING NEEDS

The first prerequisite of any service is to identify those who are to be served, and, though this is more difficult, to determine as exactly as possible their needs and how they are to be met. In the last resort this final question depends on inspiration as well as on local knowledge. It may be possible through door-to-door surveys to find where old people live. It may be possible to identify their needs in a way which fits the perception of both the old people and social workers. But when one tries to meet that need no-one may really know the answer. It is one thing for an old person—or anyone else—to feel lonely, and even to define a need for companionship, but how does one create an administrative structure that will meet so personal and yet so vital a need? It may be possible by understanding and experience to avoid the grosser mistakes, but even the old person herself is only likely to be able to identify what she does *not* want: to conceptualise the exact service required lies beyond her or anyone else simply because it is so intangible. One cannot buy human relationships by the yard.

The first requirement then, was to identify the whereabouts of old people in need, and to make sure that they knew where to seek help if and when they wanted it.* The first of these was achieved through surveys (which were sometimes eschewed on the grounds that they might uncover more needs than

* For a breakdown of methods of contact used by different groups see Appendix 2, Table A2.

a newly-formed group could deal with), through lists held by existing welfare organisations, churches, etc., and through publicity aimed at both potential referring organisations and the general public by means of posters and leaflets, sometimes containing a tear-off slip for people to indicate either needs or offers of help. (This was not always successful; a superfluity of volunteers, or a failure to match volunteers' offers with help required, could lead to disillusionment and in one case resulted in the collapse of a group.)

The second stage, of making sure that the group was notified when an old person needed help, entailed both an intensification of publicity and creating channels of communication between the group and referring bodies (welfare agencies, churches, neighbours, milkmen, etc., and old people themselves). Three groups had prepaid postcards printed and distributed to old people, either in the course of visiting or with Christmas parcels. The purpose of the card was not always understood; sometimes it would be stood on the mantelpiece and pointed out to visitors as if it were a kind of membership card; still more frustrating were the times when old people sent off cards without filling in their own names and addresses on the other side. Nevertheless, the groups who used this method considered it was worthwhile.

Problems were likely to be most acute, however, when old people were unable to get to a pillar-box, because of ill-health. Various schemes were tried to overcome this. Two groups appointed street wardens to keep an eye on old people in their immediate vicinity. Others tried to establish contact with tradesmen and others who visited people in their homes—milkmen, window cleaners, postmen and so on. These contacts were difficult to establish and maintain, especially with city-based organisations whose employees were frequently moved about from one area to another: in these situations they often preferred to report cases they found to the city old people's welfare committee office, though even there not many referrals were received. Sometimes, too, it was possible to make contact with local shopkeepers who noticed when regular customers failed to appear. In particular, one group involved the sub-postmaster who cashed most of the local people's pensions each week, and was invaluable as an information-point and 'early-warning system'.

SERVICES OFFERED

The services provided by care groups varied a great deal, according to both the needs of the area and the resources available to the group. An outline of the range of groups' activities is shown in Table 3.

Once again, various factors are involved. Some services, such as Clifton's meals-on-wheels, were a response to the specific needs of an area (Clifton is the only part of the city not covered by the WRVS meals-on-wheels service). Some are probably more a reflection of resources available to the group, or contacts built up by some group with outside organisations such as hospitals. Some services, such as visiting and various types of practical help are well-nigh universal.

TABLE 3

Services developed by care groups

Nature of service	*Number of groups offering service*
Visiting	13
Hospital visiting	3
Post-hospital care	6
Meals-on-wheels	1
Weekend meals	2
Lunch clubs	6
Over-sixty clubs started	3
Day centre	1
Keep-fit classes	2
Christmas parcels	6
Gardening, decorating, etc.	11
Shopping and other errands	8
Total care groups	14

Note:

1 This list is probably not complete; often it was difficult to determine exact responsibility for inaugurating some services, such as over-sixty clubs.

2 For a break-down by care groups see Appendix 2, Table A3.

Clearly some of these projects were much easier to run than others. A small band of trained volunteers can start a visiting service, needing little more by way of external resources than good relations with appropriate health and welfare services. Likewise, practical help can be given by anyone with a knowledge of decorating or gardening—and, equally important, an understanding of the commitment involved once a job has been started. Often these jobs led to the creation of links between care groups and schools, both strengthening the group and giving the school a local point of contact to which they could report social or medical needs that they discovered in the course of their work but were unable to meet themselves. On the financial side, arrangements were made between the OPWC and the DHSS for materials to be provided if the old people concerned were eligible for help from the department; indeed one consequence of this arrangement was for many referrals of such cases to come from DHSS staff themselves.

These, then, were fairly straightforward projects; others, such as the Meadows day centre or the Clifton meals-on-wheels service, involved considerable expense, a high level of commitment from a lot of volunteers, and co-operation with a wide range of services. It is not, therefore, surprising that such projects were undertaken only by well-established groups which had built up both resources and confidence through earlier, simpler schemes.

Finally, one type of service deserves mention because it is of a slightly different type: the distribution of Christmas parcels. The prime rationale for care groups taking on this job is their role as co-ordinator of local services; simply put, it was hoped by this means to reduce, if not eliminate, the situation in which some old people might receive half-a-dozen parcels at Christmas, while others did not get any. What began as a co-ordinating exercise, however, was always in danger of turning into a major fund-raising and administrative project, tying up scarce resources for anything up to two months before Christmas. Care groups often developed an ambivalent attitude towards this, deploring the scale of the exercise but valuing both the links with old people that it created and the wider publicity and support which it brought to the group.

WORKING WITH OTHERS

Residents

What effect have care groups had, or can they be expected to have, on the neighbourhood within which they function? Answers must be speculative. It is true that sometimes care group representatives have asked neighbours to help individual old people, especially during illness, but would they have done so anyway? It could well be correct to argue that the very existence of a care group creates an atmosphere in which people are more aware of the needs of the elderly—both through organisations such as churches or schools which are directly involved in care group activities, and as others hear about the group from friends or children, or see posters or read about the group in the local papers. But does this greater awareness of need lead to action? Or does it lead to a greater self-consciousness when helping other people, or even, as was sometimes argued, to a sense that other people are responsible now, and that the individual no longer needs to bother? Although one may assume—and certainly hope—that the influence on the neighbourhood is positive, there is no real evidence of this, and indeed it would require a long-term research programme to start to establish what effects the care groups have had on neighbourhood norms.

Groups

What we can say is that a large number of local groups have been involved in care group activities. An outline of this involvement is indicated in Table 4. Again, statistical evidence is slight both in extent and in value, and it must be remembered that we are describing a dynamic situation in which the number of contacts made by a care group is likely to increase over time.

The significance of these contacts will vary. Some groups, such as schools, are likely to be undertaking some definite piece of activity. Others, such as over-sixty clubs, may be just attending meetings of the care group as a means of 'co-ordination'—which in this context probably implies little more than keeping in touch with what each other are doing; here too, however, individual members of the club may be involved in visiting housebound old people.

Churches

It will be seen that every care group has contact with churches and indeed they are likely to be the most significant voluntary organisation at local level: there are a lot of them in most areas (other than some housing estates), they have buildings for meetings and in the person of their priest or minister they may employ the only 'professional' person to live in the neighbourhood. This can mean quite a lot in terms of having someone who is used to chairing meetings and understands committee procedure, and who probably possesses basic administrative skills which may be rare at the start of a group's existence. He will also have a status in the local community which is likely to enable him to take the lead in movements without any suggestion of 'pushing in'.

In addition, the church, even if declining, is still likely to contain a large pool of potential volunteers, though against this must be set the organisational demands of the church itself, which are often heavy and inevitably tended to fall on the 'activists' in the congregation.

Church involvement could, of course, have weaknesses as well as strengths, and it was sometimes felt that an over-dependence on churches by the care groups could deter non-church goers from participating in what they might perceive as a church-based organisation. Evidence for or against such suggestions is hard to produce, but the history of the Mapperley Churches Good Neighbour Scheme illustrates one danger. This was set up as a venture in ecumenical co-operation, and as such had an importance for the member churches over and above the practical value of the work actually carried out.

TABLE 4

Statutory and voluntary bodies involved in or in contact with care groups

Organisation	*No. of groups with which involved*
(a) *Statutory*	
Welfare services department	12
Health department	
mental welfare	4
health visitor	4
home nurse	7
home help	3
Children's department	4
Hospital medical social workers	7
General practitioners	4
Department of Health and Social Security	2
Probation department	3
(b) *Voluntary—city-wide*	
Old People's Welfare Committee	14
WRVS	5
British Red Cross Society	2
Guild for the Disabled	2
University or Colleges of Education (social service groups)	7
(c) *Voluntary—local*	
Churches	14
Youth groups	8
Schools	10
Over-sixty clubs	11
Community associations	7
Tenants'/residents' associations	6
Total no. of care groups	14

Notes:

1 In this, as in other tables, 'care groups' usually includes the old people's welfare section of wider neighbourhood groups such as the Meadows Group, rather than the larger body.

2 For a break-down of these figures by care groups see Appendix 2, Tables A4 and A5.

A large number of volunteers offered to undertake various types of task; unfortunately these did not match the requests for help, the morale of 'unemployed' volunteers gradually crumbled, and eventually the scheme collapsed. While it may be that the scheme would have failed anyway—Mapperley is a prosperous suburb in which people are not used to asking their neighbours for help—it can be argued that it had particular problems because it was an inter-church exercise. Since the success of the scheme was regarded as an indicator of the success of ecumenical co-operation, when it first ran into difficulties too much was at stake for the scheme to be dismantled and start again, or to involve outside groups who might have provided the services requested by those in need.

Community associations and tenants' associations

There have been community associations in Nottingham for many years and during the period of the project there were twenty-three associations in various parts of the city. As we have seen, there have often been close links between community associations and care groups, but co-operation has not always been easy to achieve. An inevitable problem with any group which sets out to serve the whole community within which it operates is that it will possibly assume that because it already exists there is no need for any other community group in that neighbourhood. Indeed, the existence of another group could appear to challenge the legitimacy of its claim to be in some way 'representative' of the neighbourhood. Some community associations thus regarded suggestions for the creation of care groups in their neighbourhoods as either unnecessary ('We do that kind of thing anyway') or as a possible threat, and it often took some time to break down this attitude. Others, such as Sherwood, were able to get round this problem by making the care group a sub-committee of the association. In other areas again, a fruitful and co-operative arrangement existed between the two, though even in these cases community associations could, perhaps rightly, become worried about their own identity and role. It was sometimes suggested that their role should be mainly educational and cultural, but not all associations were prepared to accept the limitations which such a role implied.

The position with tenants' and residents' associations was rather different. On the whole they saw their function mainly in terms of protecting the interests and particularly the homes of their members (who might be construed as everyone living within their area). Thus associations of council tenants might be concerned with rents or maintenance and repairs, while residents' associations could be formed to safeguard people's interests in the face of proposals for slum clearance or major road-building programmes. As such some of these groups tended to have a self-contained existence, and were sometimes suspicious of outside organisations, which were seen at various levels of sophistication as threats to autonomy and local initiative, or, more crudely, as representatives of 'them'. Again, as with community associations, tenants' and residents' groups spilled over into other activities. Some of the tenants of a new corporation housing estate, for example, became aware of the needs of elderly people who had been moved out there and approached the OPWC development officer for guidance as to how to help them.

Relations between community groups operating in the same neighbourhood are likely to give rise to certain problems, especially if one or more of them sees its role as reflecting the needs and concerns of all the people in the area. Such a group cannot easily accept limitations on its activities, since its whole *raison d'être* implies a readiness to take up whatever issues emerge from the local community. Some of these points will be discussed in Part III when we examine the idea of legitimacy. Meanwhile, we must recognise that problems are likely to arise between community groups which will not be quickly solved on a 'who does what best?' basis because of the wide-reaching terms of reference adopted by both groups. In this respect all-embracing bodies on the pattern of the Meadows Group are more likely to come into conflict with other bodies than are those on the Sherwood model with their much more clearly delimited sphere of activities.

Other social services

We have already seen in Table 4 that a number of statutory and voluntary bodies had contact with care groups, and in many cases attended their meetings. As we would expect, the services most frequently involved were those which had direct responsibilities for the elderly—the welfare services department, various divisions of the health department, the WRVS and so on. As we have seen earlier, many of these contacts reflected the efforts made by individual care groups to involve these bodies. Such contacts needed constant renewal because of changes in personnel in the social services: this seemed particularly true in the case of medical social workers. Contacts between care groups and social work agencies tended to be of two kinds: working relationships between care group organisers and individual social workers, and actual attendance at meetings. In this respect it was generally found that professional social workers were more likely to attend day-time than evening meetings, though it should be mentioned that staff of the welfare services department frequently attended care group meetings, despite the fact that there were only four welfare officers covering the entire city during most of the project. (They were supplemented, during the last two years of the project, with four welfare assistants.)

One service which is notable for its lack of contact with care groups is general medical practice. General practitioners often seem to find it difficult to attend meetings because of their hours of work, but in addition few care groups managed to establish working relationships either. One can speculate whether this is peculiar to care groups or whether it is part of a wider problem of communication between social workers and the medical profession. It should also be mentioned on the other hand that one group came into being on the initiative of a doctor's wife who was concerned about services for geriatric patients. As a consequence of her representations the local executive council agreed to her husband running a regular geriatric clinic for one half day a week.*

Finally, as an alternative means of showing the resources mobilised by care groups, Table 5 shows referrals made by the three care groups who provided the data for Table 2: the same limitations of the material should be borne in mind and it will be noted that the same variations are to be found between the groups. The table gives some indication, however, of the spread of action by the three groups, and it is worth noting that although many referrals were made to (presumably) appropriate agencies, by far the largest number of actions were taken by the group. In addition most of these cases would have involved a preliminary assessment visit, in itself a time-consuming job requiring sensitivity, observation and a knowledge of services available.

Co-ordination and co-operation

In establishing care groups considerable stress was usually laid on the importance of 'co-ordination' based on the very reasonable argument that when there were limited resources available for helping old people it was important that they should be deployed as effectively as possible. One means of achieving this was by ensuring that agencies were not overlapping and were working towards common goals. Such an attitude is, as we have seen, central to the idea of community organisation, and has been a commonplace of social policy since the 1909 Poor Law Report and the establishment of the first councils of social service.

'Co-ordination' can mean different things to different organisations, and we shall distinguish between *co-ordination*, in which the co-ordinator has power to enforce arrangements, voluntary *co-operation* in which independent groups agree on schemes to avoid overlap, and *discussions* at meetings of bodies like OPWCS which serve the purpose of informing representatives of what each other are doing, and which may therefore lead to informal co-operation.

* This scheme later ran into difficulties over problems of transport.

TABLE 5

Action taken by three care groups on first referral of an old person in need, 1969

Action taken	*Clifton*	*Meadows*	*Sherwood*	*Total*
(1) *Referred to other agency*				
(a) *Statutory*				
GP	2	2	—	4
Home help department	2	10	3	15
Health department	—	4	2	6
Mental welfare department	—	3	1	4
Welfare services department	2	8	3	13
Hospital	—	4	—	4
DHSS	1	1	—	2
Housing department	—	4	1	5
Total statutory referrals	7	36	10	53
(b) *Voluntary*				
Over-sixty clubs	—	2	2	4
Other clubs (including lunch clubs)	3	5	8	16
Churches	2	—	—	2
NOPWC	1	4	—	5
Total voluntary referrals	6	11	10	27
(2) *Action by care group*				
Visitor arranged	8	17	5	30
Sitting-in arranged	—	2	—	2
Practical help arranged	3	12	4	19
Home prepared (hospital discharge)	—	2	—	2
Meals-on-wheels arranged	13	2	—	15
Holiday arranged	1	—	—	1
Transport arranged	1	1	2	4
Care group day centre	—	15	—	15
Christmas parcel	1	—	39	40
Assessment (no action)	1	20	4	25
Neighbour asked to help	1	4	—	5
Miscellaneous	2	9	4	15
Total care group action	31	84	58	173
Total all action	44	131	78	253

Note: In some cases more than one action may have been taken for the same person.

By these definitions, it was clearly not possible for care groups to enforce co-ordination. On the other hand, we can identify examples of co-operation, such as mutual arrangements to avoid overlapping in the distribution of Christmas parcels. Only the Meadows Group, however, reached the stage of arranging case conferences between various agencies—the welfare services department, health visitors, home helps, the group itself—to try to ensure common policies. These meetings were valuable; although case conferences are common in such fields as child care, they are rare in old people's welfare. The Meadows' experience showed that different agencies in touch with the same elderly person were often not aware of each other's interest, and as a result of discussing cases it was possible to decide on common plans of action. It may be that the establishment of a combined local authority social services department may help such concerted action in the future, but case conferences could be seen as an important contribution which could be made by care groups—if they are accepted in this role by statutory social services.

The third element, that of discussion, was of course common to all groups. Simply by bringing different bodies concerned with the elderly together at local level care groups provided the opportunity for these organisations to know what each other were doing, and to frame common policies for their areas. This in itself was of value, though wider effectiveness depended on the willingness of the constituent organisations to work together to a common end.

CARE GROUP ACTIVITIES NOT CONNECTED WITH OLD PEOPLE'S WELFARE

As we have seen, some care groups have either taken responsibility for activities concerned with other groups besides old people or have been part of a larger group with that responsibility. Sometimes, as in the case of the Meadows or Clifton, the care group grew out of a parent body with a wider concern for the needs of the area as a whole. In the case of the St Ann's Tenants' and Residents' Association, a body which started in a fairly militant way to protect the interests of local people in the face of corporation redevelopment proposals gradually found itself taking on many of the functions of a care group as it became involved with the problems of elderly people awaiting rehousing. For other groups, involvement in caring for other sections of the community arose out of their work with old people—if in the course of a survey to discover housebound old people members of the group came across handicapped people who were also confined to their homes, for example, then they might try to help them as well as elderly people.

In all, half the care groups undertook wider activities of one kind or another.

Five of these were part of larger groups concerned about the needs of their areas as a whole, and the other two were becoming concerned with the needs of families and in one case of handicapped people.

In general, it was the policy of the development officer to encourage these wider activities even in those cases where initially there was no move to help the elderly. This policy was influenced by the belief that any type of community initiative was likely to lead in time to concern for old people and because it was felt unrealistic to separate the needs and interests of the elderly from those of the rest of the community. Another factor which shaped this policy was the determination of local organisations—churches, community associations and others—to involve themselves with the needs of the community as a whole. The development officer was undoubtedly helped by his position within the framework of the council of social service, which made possible links with other community action.

CARE GROUPS AS PRESSURE GROUPS

When we described community development we suggested that one of the valid 'self-help' activities which a neighbourhood could undertake was to demand resources and services from those who controlled them. If this is so, and if groups have been successful, then we might expect that care group activities would have led to an increased demand for and provision of services for the elderly in their neighbourhood. Evidence of this, other than those services established by care groups with local authority finance, is scant. Certainly in some areas the demand has increased, particularly for some of the domiciliary services such as home helps; what is less clear is how far there has been an increase in provision, and if so whether this has been in consequence of care group activities, of better publicity leading to a higher demand from old people themselves, or simply because the corporation has had more money to spend on services.

Yet although clear examples may be hard to come by, this aspect of care groups should not be under-rated. Their formation has created a large body of people who are both concerned and informed about the needs of old people and of their neighbourhood as a whole. Even if they have not often made general demands to the local authority for more extensive and appropriate services, their activities have undoubtedly increased the total demand for these services in a way that the authority will find difficult to ignore. And meanwhile a body of opinion is building up at local level which will be appreciative of increases in the provision of local services when they come about, even if it means higher rates.

It should not be assumed that in acting as pressure groups care committees will incur the wrath of the authorities. Such outside pressure may be of help to those inside the corporation who are themselves pressing for more resources. It is, in fact, a recognition of the way in which democracy works, and a means of making known the needs of a section of the community which is often inarticulate and unheard.

CHAPTER 5

The Administration of Care Groups

WHO RUNS THE CARE GROUPS?

In the previous chapter we have mentioned the neighbourhood and city-based organisations which provided much of the membership of care groups. What this does not show, however, are the members of care groups who were not connected with any other organisation, nor, which is perhaps more significant, does it indicate the strength of support which came from the various members of groups. After all, membership of care groups was in many cases a pretty amorphous affair—it might represent those who were actually voluntary workers, it might derive from an open and general meeting advertised in the neighbourhood, or it might depend on a haphazard mailing list, built up over time with the names of anyone who was thought to be interested in the group's aims. On the other hand, there was usually a small central core of workers whose labour was essential to the continued existence of the group. While these core workers were not always the officers of the group, the investment of time and effort by the officers and particularly by the secretary/organisers was very considerable. It is worth starting, therefore, by considering where these people came from: were they local residents, or from outside the area, did they come to care groups as members of some other organisation or was the group their only commitment?

Table 6 gives a limited answer to some of these questions. In particular it indicates that in general the only strong 'professional' group holding office in care groups were clergymen, and this supports our earlier discussion about their importance (see page 38). The other major factor is the indication of the number of local residents who have become involved in running care groups. This has helped to anchor the groups firmly to their locality, and is an indication of the way in which it is possible to find local leadership. A third point worth mentioning is the small but important group of non-indigenous volunteers in some areas, particularly at an early stage, when it was difficult to attract volunteers from the locality; outsiders could on occasion be a tower of strength.

TABLE 6

Officers of care groups by background

Background	*Chairman*	*Secretary*	*Treasurer*	*Total*
Clergyman	8	3	0	11
Local resident	4	10	3	17
Non-local volunteer	2	1	0	3

Notes:
1 Most groups did not have an official treasurer.
2 For a break-down by care groups, see Appendix 2, Table A6.

Despite the efforts of these voluntary workers, however, some groups found it necessary (or at any rate desirable, funds being available) to employ staff on a part-time or full-time basis. Some groups have paid an honorarium for certain services, notably to the lunch club organiser at Sherwood. Two groups also had full-time workers. Of these one, working in the St Ann's area, was a community worker financed by the United Nations Association.* In the Meadows two successive workers had been employed on 'full-time volunteer' rates (i.e. an allowance for board and lodging plus pocket money); subsequently the group obtained a two-year grant from the NCCOP to employ a salaried community worker. The application was made on the grounds of the particular needs of the area and of the extent of the group's activities. One could foresee that, if funds were available, other groups might in time seek to make similar appointments.

ADMINISTRATIVE FUNCTIONS

For a care group to function certain administrative tasks needed to be performed, over and above the activities described in Chapter 4. These were directed first to the maintenance and cohesion of the group itself, second to the maintenance of links with other organisations, and third to servicing the group's activities.

Maintaining the group

The group needed to be maintained in a number of ways. First of these was the allocation of tasks. If members (individuals or organisations) were not given jobs to do, their interest and enthusiasm was likely to flag and they would eventually drop out: we have seen how this happened at Mapperley. On the

* Finance of this project was later taken over by Christian Aid.

other hand, they might become resentful if they felt they were being overworked, with equally disastrous results.

Secondly members needed supporting in the work which they performed. This might involve no more than a periodic enquiry by the organiser as to how they were getting on (which also served the function of ensuring that their elderly client was still receiving help) but it could also involve taking up and passing on specific needs which required the aid of some other agency. It also usually involved general meetings for voluntary workers which served a dual function of training and creating group cohesion. This in its turn involved the organiser in keeping up to date with wider issues which would be of interest to members of the group.

Thirdly, the group needed to be maintained by regular 'business' meetings, at which matters of policy and organisation were discussed. Here again it was important to provide people with a sense of belonging to the organisation and having a say in what took place, though without letting meetings, or indeed any aspect of administration, become an end in itself, so that the group simply degenerated into a talking shop. Meetings might include routine business, decisions about future plans, and discussions of wider issues affecting old people or the community as a whole. One group which covered a peripheral housing estate which was thought to receive inadequate public services invited a succession of speakers from various services such as the police and the corporation transport department to discuss with them the needs of their area. In this way the group managed to maintain something of the character of a 'community forum', while at the same time providing definite and practical services through its other activities.

Fourthly, the maintenance of the group involved a constant awareness of the needs for expansion: a static group soon started to slip backwards. There was thus a need to maintain a positive recruiting policy, to seek publicity for the group, address meetings and forge links with an ever-widening circle of organisations and individuals able to assist with its work.

Liaison with other bodies

Reference has already been made to the importance of maintaining contact with other organisations, particularly at city level, and we have seen the effect which, for example, the Meadows Group's contact with hospital medical social workers had on the number of cases referred to them from this source. The maintenance and expansion of these links involved not just contacts through meetings but also through establishing working relationships, and re-establishing them when there was a change of personnel.

This would involve the organiser in attending meetings of other organisations. These might be local social workers' lunch clubs, at which relationships could be formed and fostered. It might also mean attendance at city-based organisations, particularly meetings of the old people's welfare committee, which provided a link between the care groups and other bodies, such as corporation departments, and could combine the representations of individual care groups into general policy requests for the whole city.*

Servicing activities: general

This is in part the other side of the support of voluntary workers which we have already mentioned. If care groups were to serve old people adequately then some check needed to be made to ensure that they continued to receive care. From this arose the need to keep records: lists of old people receiving regular help, of those who required or received occasional help, such as Christmas parcels, and of those who were 'at risk'—the housebound, people living alone, and those who were very frail. Parallel lists of volunteers and of other sources of help were also needed. The standard and sophistication of record keeping varied. Some groups had card-indexes derived from surveys of the whole area, while at the other extreme the group's entire records may have existed in a couple of notebooks. Clearly much depended on the size of the operation, and the resources available to the group.

A further aspect of administration, and one which varied in complexity, arose from the need for the public to have clearly identifiable ways of getting in touch with the group. Many groups put up posters or pushed handbills through letter-boxes, informing local people of the group's existence, but these led to the need for one or more contact points—an address or telephone number at which people could request help. Sometimes this would be the secretary's own home, perhaps supplemented with the addresses of some voluntary workers spread across the district, in other cases it included community centres or churches. This could create problems for the workers involved: it is desirable that people should be able to call for help quickly, but this could mean that those involved were on call twenty-four hours a day, seven days a week, which might place them under severe strain.

Table 7 gives some indication of the variety of location of administration.

Servicing special activities

We have already seen that some groups were responsible for quite ambitious schemes—Sherwood's lunch club, the Meadows day centre, Clifton's meals-on-wheels scheme. Such projects required a lot of time from whoever was

* Although in no sense 'compulsory', most groups joined the OPWC once they had become firmly established.

running them, and stress was placed on giving this responsibility to people or organisations other than the secretary of the group, so that he or she could be free for the general concerns of the group, including looking out for new needs and ways of meeting them. Some groups, particularly Sherwood, also tried to hive off responsibility for visiting services, since these too could be very time-consuming, but these services were so closely inter-related with other aspects of the group's activities and membership that it was found difficult for the secretary not to be closely involved.

TABLE 7

Location of administrative services of care groups

Location	*Focal point*	*Admin. base*	*Committee meeting place*
Church/vicarage	5	3	9
Community centre	2	3	5
Own home	8	9	–
Other (e.g. shop)	3	1	1

Notes:

1 Some groups had more than one base—especially for focal points.

2 For a breakdown of these figures by care groups see Appendix 2, Table A7.

ADMINISTRATION: RESOURCES

Personnel

As we have already seen, the secretary was a crucial figure. The danger was for him (or her) to be completely overwhelmed with work, and for the activities of the group to suffer as a result. There was also the problem of secretaries becoming too indispensable and then leaving, with no-one well informed enough to take over.

A possible solution was the decentralisation of responsibility, by such methods as the encouragement of permanent organisations in the area (churches, schools, community associations) to take on responsibility for some aspects of administration. This had the additional advantage of involving more local people in the scheme, and possibly leading them on to more active involvement in the care of the elderly. The typing and duplicating of minutes by the schools in the Meadows and the administrative support given by community associations in Sherwood and Broxtowe are examples of this principle. Attempts were also made to appoint assistant secretaries with responsibilities for specific aspects of the work. The main problem with this kind of decentralisation is that the work of the secretary can in fact increase as he tries to draw together the various threads of administration.

Material aids

These can be dealt with more briefly. Although a meeting place was important, it was rare for churches or community centres not to make a room available and problems only arose in this respect on new estates lacking communal meeting rooms. More important was the kind of office equipment that most social services take for granted but are not always common in private houses—stationery, filing cabinets, card-indexes, money for postage, a duplicating machine, perhaps a typewriter, certainly a telephone. It would have been unreasonable—and perhaps disastrous—to have expected a secretary to provide these things from his own pocket.

Finance

The finance required by care groups varied considerably. General running costs—postage, stationery and the like—might come to only £5 or £10 per annum, though a telephone would increase this figure. But special projects, whether Christmas parcels or some more substantial piece of work, could involve a group in considerable expense very quickly, and carried with it the danger of fund-raising absorbing too much of the group's energy—though it could, in short, successful bursts, also lead to the encouragement and cohesion of the groups. Table 8 shows how groups have raised money. Local authority grants were usually made for specific services such as lunch clubs, but some of the larger care groups were also successful in general applications for grant aid. There is a strong case to be made for local authority grants for administration: this is an essential part of the care group's operations, but one for which it is not easy to make an appeal to the general public. The OPWC in most cases made a 'pump-priming' grant of £5 when groups were formed, but this usually only covered the expenses of the first few months. To continue, and to develop more ambitious schemes, required money, and indeed some groups found this a more serious problem than the recruitment of volunteers when they tried to expand. For community care schemes to succeed, this question of resources has to be faced, and in the long run it is questionable whether such bodies can reach optimum effectiveness without local authority support.

TABLE 8

Sources of care group finance

Source	*No. of groups helped for* administration	services
Local authority	3	4
Charitable trust, etc.	2	–
Nottingham OPWC	9	–
Rotary clubs	1	3
Own fund-raising		
Socials	8	
Jumble sales	5	
Prize draws	3	
Collection boxes	4	

Note: For a breakdown of these figures by care groups see Appendix 2, Table A8.

CHAPTER 6

The Role of the Worker

PHILOSOPHY: THE NON-DIRECTIVE APPROACH

Up to this point the development officer has been a rather shadowy figure, moving behind the scenes of care group activities rather than appearing in a leading role. This is likely to be the experience of anyone involved in community work, in which emphasis is placed on achievements of local residents, but it is important to see how the development officer worked to enable them to achieve these results.

First, we need to recognise the theory that guided much of the worker's activities. The non-directive method of community development starts from the viewpoint that ordinary people—those who receive social services, those who will live in the houses the corporation builds, and in the district that the planners create, whose children attend the local schools and so on—that these people should have more of a say in running their own lives, that they should be able to decide what is needed in their community, and should be helped to obtain or to create what they want. And if this is true of the services brought into their area from outside, so it is true of the services which they create for themselves, be they recreational, welfare, political or whatever: they should be able to create and direct their own institutions, rather than have a stereotyped pattern imposed on them from outside.

There are various reasons for this, theoretical and practical. At the general level, it is argued that people are responsible for their own lives, and should be treated accordingly, and that the present emphasis on 'participation' is only restoring an element of democracy that has tended to be submerged under the large-scale institutions of modern government. At a practical level there are a number of arguments. First, there is the experience of the consumers of services. In a very real sense it is true that only those who live in high blocks of flats know what it is like to do so, and this applies to all other social provisions, too. It may be legitimate for a commercial organisation to persuade people to buy their product whether they really want it or not, but in the case of a public service, consumer preference must clearly be given a very high priority, since this is after all the whole *raison d'être* of the service.

But community development goes beyond this. It does not just ask people what they want, but goes on to involve them in the provision of that service, both as voluntary workers and in having a say in policy matters. The assumption here is that people will put more into the service if they feel that it is they who control it, and in the long run the hope is that they will feel they have some control over their whole environment, and will start to react accordingly.

The practical application of this approach is that wherever possible people should be encouraged to make their own decisions, and take their own actions. The worker is there to help to clarify issues and to facilitate activities, but at no time is he in a directive role. This carries certain implications for his approach to the work and the way in which he is seen by others. To outsiders it may be hard to determine just what he is doing—if anything. He has no 'shop window' to show to passers-by; he cannot say 'I achieved this; I organised that; so many voluntary workers are at my beck and call'. Nor is it only outsiders who are perplexed by this refusal to give 'a clear lead'; there will be pressure at local level too for the worker to take command: 'You know what type of organisation works best; you can run this better than we can; you're the expert.' The worker has to explain that while he may have certain knowledge, it is not he, but they, who will have to run the group, and they must start from the outset to acquire the necessary skills. And he is not the expert on *their* area; they are.

As this develops, the worker finds himself not in the caseworker–client relationship of traditional social work, but working alongside people as a colleague and as a friend, sharing their triumphs and frustrations, imparting skills and learning lessons. His ultimate shop window is '*We* achieved this'.

Tasks

The work of the development officer can be grouped under four main headings, though naturally there was often overlap between them.* They are: developing initiatives, passing on information and skills, effecting links, and giving direct aid. With the exception of the last, the methods of performing these tasks were influenced by what we have already noted about the non-directive approach: the aim was not so much to tell people what to do as to enable them to discover it for themselves.

* A similar analysis of a community worker's job, to which this is indebted, will be found in Goetschius, G.: *Working with Community Groups*; London, Routledge and Kegan Paul, 1969.

Developing initiatives

The problems of non-directiveness were at their strongest at the start of a care group's life, when the first approaches were made. The worker had to be able to gauge which initiatives were worth following up, and which he should leave alone. Some of this would become clear in subsequent discussions with other people in the neighbourhood, but here too he had to tread a delicate path, opening up to people the possibilities that might lie before them, without creating a transient enthusiasm which might soon fade, leaving a group of embittered people carrying responsibilities which they were unwilling to discharge.

Thus, once the decision was taken that a suggested initiative was viable, the worker had to encourage without, as far as possible, actually taking the lead (though this might sometimes be necessary if, for example, the initial approach came not from someone offering help, but from someone needing it). The worker could suggest possible ways forward, pointing out the advantages and disadvantages of each. He could refer to the experience of other groups, without suggesting that this should be slavishly copied, indeed for this reason he was usually chary of introducing members of established groups into a new situation. His role was to facilitate the actions which other people wished to take, by suggesting ways in which their ideas could be put into practice, pointing out pitfalls and, if necessary, seeking to provide resources—duplicating leaflets, writing letters, etc., which were not yet within the capabilities of the local initiators. People could be encouraged at an early stage by having literature sent out beneath an 'official' letter-heading, thus perhaps providing some degree of legitimacy at this point of the group's development. The worker, in short, had to be a vehicle for other people's visions, an objective enthusiast.

Providing information and teaching skills

Initiative had to lie with the local people, but they still needed to have information and to learn basic skills, both welfare and administrative, if they were to achieve their aims. The worker thus had to become an educator, always anxious to lead on his 'students' at a pace which was appropriate to them but which all the time widened and deepened their experience, and expanded the areas of competence in which they no longer needed the worker's assistance.

But knowledge needs to be imparted carefully if the student is to retain his own initiative and not to become a pale stereotype of his tutor. As far as possible the worker had to avoid the blunt statement: 'You do it this way' and above all, 'Here, let *me* do it'. The introduction of information had therefore to be tempered to the needs of the group. At an early stage there would be factual questions to answer, simple skills to be imparted, but the group might need to be nursed and coaxed along, with the worker aware of the danger of the group accepting his suggestions too readily. In a well-established group, on the other hand, the worker could join freely in a robust debate, knowing that there were others there quite capable of matching him, and perhaps beating him in arguments, and in the experience that lay behind their ideas. This maturity developed quickly among groups; only a couple of years might separate 'Would it be worth considering, Mr Chairman . . . ?' from 'You know that's a load of old rubbish!'

The kinds of information the worker might be called on to provide would be various. Sometimes he could answer them directly: 'Where can we get money for decorating Mrs X's house?'—'Try the MSS; the PACHwork* committee may be able to help.' Often he might suggest alternative sources of information: 'What new activities can our over-sixty club try?'—'Have you seen what they're doing at Basford? Why not talk to Mrs Y?' Sometimes they might involve creating a link with another agency. 'I'm worried about Mrs Z; I'm sure she's mentally ill'—'Have you talked to the Mental Health Department? Would you like their phone number? Ask for Mr A.'

Sometimes, if he felt the moment was right, the worker might take the initiative in feeding in information—'Have you heard what they're doing in Clifton? Would it be worth going to see what's happening in Hull?' Circulars were sent out, too, giving information which could be of use to all groups, perhaps containing information about new services offered by the city welfare services department or the Department of Health and Social Security.

From time to time informal meetings were held between members of different care groups, to give people an opportunity to swap ideas. Members of care groups also got the chance to meet one another at training courses for voluntary workers in old people's welfare. Examples of these included a series of ten weekly talks by members of appropriate departments on services available for the elderly, and an annual three-day residential conference organised jointly with the Nottinghamshire OPWC. These training courses at once imparted direct information, and gave people a chance for the informal exchange of experience. We are thus led naturally on to our third section.

Effecting links

One of the major images used by the council of social service and its associated

* PACHwork—Practical Action Clearing House; a central body for 'young volunteer' projects.

bodies in describing their work was that of linking various inter-related networks. The pattern was seen as a series of horizontal networks—at neighbourhood level, at city level, at national level; welfare networks, cultural networks, political networks, economic and industrial networks through which rose a series of vertical links of 'needs groups' and 'interest groups' linking what was going on at the grass-roots with what was happening at city level, and beyond. The whole model thus ended up looking something like a milk-crate,* with the horizontal wires representing geographical and 'across the board' networks, and verticals representing particular interests. To take a simple example, a local music group might have links at local ('horizontal') level with other music groups, with the church whose hall they used for rehearsals, with the school which helped sell programmes for them, with the shops which displayed their posters, and with the women's institute to which half of the members also belonged. Their 'vertical' links could include the City Arts Association, various regional festivals, and national affiliation to the English Folk Dance and Song Society. But communications were not always as good as this, and the council of social service saw as its task the creation and strengthening of links within and between these various networks, particularly between those who would not normally have been on the same network, but who might still co-operate to mutual advantage. To go back to our previous example, there might be a music group looking for a meeting place and a community centre anxious to increase their activities—could they be linked together? Or links could be effected at individual level: chance remarks over the tea-table introduced someone interested in teaching adults to read to someone else who had experience of such a scheme run by a London settlement.

With this kind of approach, and backed by a federal organisation determined to latch on to as many networks as possible, it is understandable that the development officer attached considerable importance to this part of his work. Links could be of four kinds—between individuals and groups, between groups and other services and organisations, between different groups, and within groups.

Between individuals and groups: However hard care groups might try it was difficult for them to become widely known outside their own areas. The worker was thus frequently contacted by outside agencies wishing to make referrals to a care group, such as hospitals discharging elderly patients, or by old people themselves who wanted some kind of help. Quite a lot of time could be spent on these referrals, and the worker might have to assess whether a newly-formed group was capable of taking on a case. It could also be

* See Appendix 3 for a diagram of this concept.

possible, of course, to use these enquiries to create direct links between welfare agencies and care groups.

Between groups and other services: Not only did outside services need to be informed of care groups' existence, but there was also a need for links in the other direction. Care group workers needed to know what services were offered by, for example, the various corporation departments concerned with welfare, and, perhaps equally important, the correct person to contact. Professional social workers with experience of local authorities sometimes forget just how difficult it is for an amateur to find his way through the maze of what he may previously have thought of vaguely and without differentiation as 'the Corporation'. At times information about an official might be enough; in other circumstances the worker might effect a personal introduction.

Links were not just limited to the welfare and health departments; they could also include the housing, planning, cleansing and transport departments and organisations outside the corporation.

Between care groups: These links have been discussed in the previous section (page 57).

Within care groups: As the worker became known within the group he was often brought in to try to resolve tensions and conflicts between members. Sometimes this involved little more than clarifying what someone had meant to say, at other times it could involve the worker in quite protracted negotiations. Work of this nature arose in part from the identification of the worker as a colleague within the care group, yet at the same time someone sufficiently distinct from it, and whose standing derived from an organisation other than the care group: he could thus be trusted to take an objective approach to problems when someone whose whole loyalty was to the care group could have found it difficult not to take sides.

Direct assistance

Although, as we have seen, the emphasis was usually placed on care groups doing things for themselves, there were occasions when the worker gave direct assistance. These were usually when a group needed help to carry them over a particular difficulty or when the task concerned was relevant for a number of different care groups. Examples of the former could be seen in the inauguration of groups, perhaps in duplicating literature or arranging meetings or providing initial financial help. The worker might also add his support when a project seemed too much for a group although in the long run it would benefit them: he thus helped with surveys carried out by the Meadows and Clifton groups. In such situations it was important that he should be seen as just another helper.

An example of the second type of help, in which the worker took an active part because of repercussions for a number of groups, also arises from Clifton, in which the worker participated in a small survey of old people in a block of flats who were having trouble with under-floor heating. This was clearly a problem which could affect old people all over the city, and so it was appropriate that the OPWC should be involved and make representations to the electricity board. A simpler example of joint action from the centre was when the worker made an application on the part of all the care groups who wished to do so to make a street collection for Christmas parcels for old people.

SKILLS

From the description of the worker's task we can go on to suggest certain skills which someone in this kind of post is likely to require. Some of these will be in the field of human relations, some imply an ability to assess and interpret a situation, some will involve communication, and some will be administrative. Most of these skills will presuppose certain types of knowledge.

Human relations

This is a vague term, and even when we have analysed some of the situations in which this expertise is needed we may not be able to say much more than that a worker must be able to get on with people. But we can at least identify some of the settings: with individuals, with small groups, in formal meetings. In every case the worker must be able to understand other people, to recognise their strengths and weaknesses and to react accordingly. There will be times when he will need to enthuse people and jolly them along, and there will be other occasions when he must recognise that fundamental problems exist which must not be glossed over. He must learn to identify factions within larger groups and try to use them in a constructive fashion and he must be aware of the ways in which people may try to enlist his support in their own private struggles.

Nor will these skills only be necessary in care groups themselves. There will be people outside the group, perhaps professional social workers or members of a community association, who feel threatened by the new development and need to be reassured. And the worker will also need to retain the skills of the social worker dealing with individual old people. However much further he may develop other skills he is still likely to be called on to deal with or advise on individual cases, and indeed this is a field of expertise which he will need in order to impart it to the groups with which he works.

The ability to assess and interpret situations

The worker needs to be able to understand and interpret what is happening in a community, and in a care group, and to assess its value. He thus needs some understanding of the way in which change takes place in society or in small groups. This also means that he must be aware of the social make-up of a given area, and of the factors within the social situation which are likely to lead to change, whether very rapidly such as when redevelopment plans are implemented, or slowly as when a 'respectable' neighbourhood gradually becomes a 'twilight zone', or as the average age on a council estate slowly rises.

In understanding these factors he will come to know which of them are reversible or capable of being channelled along particular lines, and he will be able to assess whether such planned change is feasible and if so who should be asked to do it. This might, in the case of our second example, involve making representations to the housing department, requesting modifications to their existing lettings policies, or to the welfare department pointing out that the demographic changes may demand a greater concentration of resources in a given area. And in all cases it will involve helping the local community to understand what is going on, and to enable them to formulate their own wishes and to make them known.

What is true on a large scale will also be true in the context of a group or between individuals: again, the worker must be able to interpret what is going on, explain this to others, and if necessary seek to modify what is happening. This brings us back again to skills in personal relationships.

Communication

It is not enough for a worker to be able to understand what is going on, he must also be able to communicate it to others. We have seen in the previous section the importance of imparting information and effecting links between different groups, and the natural corollary of this is that the worker must be able to communicate his knowledge. Communication skills are obvious enough, but the worker must be able to adapt his style to his audience: he must be able to speak to small and large groups, to write committee memoranda, newsletters and posters—or at any rate to know someone who can.

Administration

It is easy to assume that the worker spent all his time in the field, but often he was in fact in his office, and this became increasingly necessary as schemes grew in number and size. There were letters to be written, referrals to be passed on, committees to be serviced and records to be kept. All these required time and resources, as well as skills. This point does not need labouring, particularly since we revert to it in the following section, in which we describe the context in which the worker performed his task.

THE WORK SITUATION

The development officer did not exist in isolation. He was part of an organisation which had responsibility for a wide range of social work activities, and this naturally was reflected in the way in which his own work developed. He himself assumed other responsibilities, and he received help from his colleagues. In addition, his style of operation was influenced by the growing number of groups with which he was connected.

First, however, we look at practical details. The worker, like care group organisers, needed an administrative base from which to work—in this case an office in the CSS premises in the centre of town. This was a point at which he could be contacted, where he could meet people, and where administrative work was done. We have already shown the extent to which administrative resources were needed for the work, and this was still more important on those occasions when care groups were unable to provide their own typing and duplicating facilities. Adequate backing-up resources are essential for developments of this nature, and administration is a cost which must be recognised from the start of any scheme.

Hours of work were long: inevitably meetings had to be held when people could manage them, and when volunteers were involved this often meant evenings and to a certain extent weekends. Although there was provision for taking time off during the day in lieu of evening work, pressure of work was such that this was seldom possible.

During the last two years of the project the development officer also acted as secretary of the OPWC following the retirement of the previous secretary. Although this was in one sense a natural development, bringing the community care work into the centre of the committee's activities, it also meant that he had to take on other tasks and that administrative responsibilities such as servicing committees and attending meetings also increased.

During this period too the style of work began to change as a result of the growing number of groups. When there were half a dozen groups the worker could devote a lot more time to each of them than when there were fourteen. Parts of this change were natural—initial teething troubles were at an end for some groups, and they were more confident in day-to-day running of their own affairs. On the other hand, they might in consequence be turning to larger schemes in which they still needed support, and meanwhile other new groups were also clamouring for attention. To give some indication of the size of the operation, in the fourth year of the project the development officer and his assistant attended 148 meetings on care group work alone. The worker had thus to become more selective in deciding how to allocate his time, while with care groups now covering a large part of the city he could start looking beyond a series of isolated groups to a total policy both as regards the spread and activities of care groups and in taking up at city level the common problems of the elderly reported by various groups.

In this he was helped by his position within the CSS. The staff included a number of people who although they had particular fields of responsibilities thought of themselves as community workers, taking a total view of community needs in the city. This support from colleagues and particularly from the general secretary of the CSS, was of considerable importance. Community work is a lonely job, and because of the intangible nature of many of the results it is often hard to assess the value of one's work. In casework, systems of supervision have been developed to help overcome some of the tensions involved, but this is rare in community work because of the scarcity of community workers who understand what one another are doing; it was not the least advantage of the work situation that the development officer was able to rely on the support of professional colleagues.

CHAPTER 7

Assessment

QUANTITATIVE

Any study of voluntary groups is likely to run up against a problem of inadequate records. On the one hand, it is understandably difficult to persuade the busy secretary of a care group of the need for accurate statistical returns, and on the other hand there are the problems associated with the intangible nature of much of the work. It is one thing to add up lists of volunteers, but it becomes much more difficult to quantify neighbourliness, though the group may be devoting much time to the promotion and support of this quality. Equally, figures of old people being helped at any given time may be only a small proportion of the total number of elderly people known to the group.

The figures that follow, therefore, are likely to give a serious underestimate of the total exercise. In particular, those for 1970 only refer to nine of the twelve care groups then in operation. Nevertheless, they may help to give some picture of the scale of the operation and of the move from a central to a neighbourhood-based operation.

TABLE 9

Numbers of volunteers and old people helped, 1965 and 1970

	volunteers employed		*old people helped*	
	1965	*1970*	*1965*	*1970*
By OPWC centrally	70	27	300	71
By care groups	60	450	180	500
Total	130	477	480	571
Number of groups for whom figures are available	3	9	3	9

Points which immediately arise, apart from the shift of emphasis, are the great increase in volunteers, and the relatively small increase in numbers of old people helped. The latter figure may well be explained in differences of classification between the OPWC who probably gave a generous estimate in 1965 of the extent of help—this figure includes, for example, people taken on coach trips once a year—and care groups, whose contacts were almost certainly much wider than this figure suggests. The figures for volunteers give an indication of the success of the project in decentralising the recruitment and deployment of voluntary workers: it would have been impossible to handle that number from a central office, even if they had offered their help.

THE NATURE OF THE SERVICE

It is not enough to indicate that so many old people were helped as a result of care group activities; we have also to ask what was the quality of the service that they received. There are a number of ways in which we can look at this; but we will concentrate on two questions: did the decentralisation of services to local level increase the likelihood of old people getting the service most appropriate for them, and was the service thus provided more or less efficient or satisfactory than it might otherwise have been? A third question, that of the impact of the scheme on local communities, has been discussed in an earlier section.

How appropriate was the service?

We have argued at various points in this report that to be effective a social service must be designed to meet the real problem of the client, rather than what the social worker or his employing agency may suppose it to be. It follows that a prerequisite of any service must be adequate communication between the client and the provider of the service. This may sound easy enough, but not all services have efficient 'upward' lines of communication, and the fragmentation of services between different agencies increases the likelihood that no-one will have responsibility for needs not at present being met by any service. There is thus a need for a proper interpretation of needs at local level, coupled with adequate feed-back to those agencies whose responsibility it is to meet them.

How well was this happening in Nottingham? To begin with, there were not many people with a sufficiently inclusive view of the needs of the elderly to be able to spot, and then follow up, unmet needs. Although a large number of agencies—home helps, health visitors, doctors, DHSS, WRVS—had certain responsibilities, they were usually concerned with some particular facet of an old person's needs, and thus were unlikely to pick up wider issues. The only statutory workers with any kind of general responsibility for the welfare of the elderly were the welfare officers attached to the welfare services department, and for most of the period of the project there were only four of them (with, later, four assistants) to cover the whole city for all types of domiciliary welfare responsibility (including the welfare of the physically handicapped).

The advantage of care groups was that they could provide a focus where needs could be reported and assessed at local level. This latter point is important since many needs were interpreted in the form of services appropriate to groups of people in the local community—for example, lunch clubs. We must ask, however, whether care groups established new services because they were stated to be needed by old people in the area or because the organisers thought that the need existed. Perhaps more common were situations in which, for practical reasons, requests from old people for one type of service were adapted according to the resources of the group: thus requests for more meals-on-wheels might lead to the establishment of a lunch club.

More fundamental is the question of how far the principle of self-determination actually extended to old people themselves. Although their membership frequently included some old people, especially from over-sixty clubs, care groups have still, by and large, been the means by which one group—the helpers—determine for another group—the helped—both their needs and methods of meeting those needs. This almost paradoxical situation is, after all, only a reflection of an attitude which exists in all the social services, and which we are only just beginning to recognise.* Hence the importance of care groups involving over-sixty clubs in their activities and discussions, since these clubs are one of the few self-help organisations largely run by the old people themselves.

Even if there were adequate consultation, however, we should not assume that every problem would thereby be solved. It is one thing to identify a need—and even this is not an easy matter, as anyone can testify who has been asked by his doctor: 'What *kind* of pain is it?'—but once diagnosis has taken place, treatment must follow, and here, as we have suggested earlier (see page 34) the sufferer may not be the best guide: treatment requires a knowledge of the remedies available, or inspiration for the location of new ones.

The provision of a service thus involves many different elements. Perhaps an example of the total process can be seen in the establishment of the Meadows day centre. Here, the original in-put—that there were a number of housebound and confused elderly people—came from a number of agencies, from

* See e.g. Meyer, J. E. and Timms, N.: *The Client Speaks*; London, Routledge and Kegan Paul, 1970.

voluntary workers, neighbours and relatives, from the old people themselves as they demanded help in various ways, and from the personal observations of the care group organiser. The next stage was to discover the best answer to the problem and this was thought to be the day centre at St Francis' Hospital. At this point, wide knowledge of services available was needed. When it was found impossible to extend the St Francis service to include all the needs in the Meadows, and no other statutory body was willing to take on responsibility, the care group decided to set up its own service.

Two further points may be mentioned. First, in this case an imaginative decision, based on a wide range of possibilities, was decided on, but we have no guarantee that this will always be so. One danger of decentralising decision-making is that local people, with inadequate knowledge of services available, or simply because of prejudice, may become committed to a service which in the eyes of professional workers may seem quite old-fashioned and even retrograde. The worker may find himself in a dilemma here between allowing the care group self-determination (and perhaps to learn from their mistakes) and to protect the old people who are also his responsibility. The educational element of his work, enabling people to make informed decisions, thus becomes very important.

The second point is the danger, again avoided in this instance, of interpreting needs in terms of available services. This can be all too easy, especially when problems are often expressed in very vague terms. This is one reason why it is important to think of care groups as pressure groups as well as providers of services: in this way they can avoid the danger of trying to mould needs to fit services and can retain the independence to assess as accurately as possible the service which will meet the need, and then see to it that someone provides it.

How effective was the service?

The effectiveness of care group services cannot be discussed in purely general terms without defining which services we are discussing. In general, the major projects—lunch clubs, meals-on-wheels, the day centre—encountered a lot of problems while they were being launched, but thereafter proved highly successful. Perhaps because of these earlier difficulties no group was going to allow such major undertakings to fail for lack of support, and in the process of launching the schemes the organisers usually became very well-informed about appropriate ways of running them.

When we turn to 'personal services' carried out by voluntary workers on a one-to-one basis it is more difficult to assess effectiveness. Some schemes were very well-organised, with regular checks and visitors' meetings at which cases were discussed and new information about services was given out. Others were less efficient and may have worked on the assumption that 'So long as we don't hear anything it's all right'. It wasn't always: visitors might have stopped calling or decorating projects could be left in the middle of a job because of school holidays, and the overworked organiser might take a long time to discover the position.

In part, these failures can be ascribed to the almost inevitable problems arising from extended lines of communication, although there was more likelihood of a check being kept by someone in the locality than by one of the two OPWC members of staff. A further difficulty could arise in those districts where people were unwilling to be recruited as 'official' volunteers, but were prepared to help a neighbour in trouble. In such a situation it was clearly inappropriate to expect the good neighbour regularly to report back on how things were going, but without this it was difficult to tell whether the old person was being cared for adequately. Such situations created dilemmas, but it may have been better to accept the imperfections of a social situation in which people were prepared to help one another rather than to insist on a standard of efficiency which excluded large sections of the local community who were potentially valuable resources and allies. Certainly it was considered in Nottingham that the gains very much outweighed the losses.

THE VALUE OF THE COMMUNITY WORK APPROACH

To close this section we recapitulate the advantages which the workers saw in their method of working:

1 Having a city-wide base, they could take up and support developments as they arose, and help to tackle problems which really concerned local people in the most flexible way within the framework of a natural neighbourhood. All these aspects maximised the potential contribution of the community.* It was untidy from an administrative point of view, and led to a variety of structures and services, but it appeared to make sense to those who actually ran the schemes 'on the ground' as the results show, and was thus an *effective* use of resources.

2 Encouraging the development of the care of the elderly as an integral part of general neighbourhood development was also a central principle. Although it could lead to ambiguity about the position of a worker supposedly concerned with old people's welfare, it had a number of advantages. It maintained links between the OPWC and neighbourhood organisations—and indeed

* A further aspect of this was to take up services which appeared most relevant for a particular community, rather than impose a standard type of service, such as visiting schemes or street wardens.

individuals and groups of secondary volunteers*—who were interested in a wide range of problems. Furthermore many of the wider problems taken up by neighbourhood groups—housing, transport, civic amenities and the like, were as important for old people as for any other members of the community. There is always a danger of segregating the elderly from the community of which they are in reality an integral part by thinking in terms of specialised services for them, and a general approach helped to counteract this tendency.

3 The emphasis on services at neighbourhood level led to the recruitment of workers who would never have thought of taking part in a city-based scheme. It built up support at local level which gave schemes the possibility of independence if at any time the OPWC had to withdraw support; and trained local leadership, realising the latent potentialities of the community, and thereby enriching the whole city.

CAN THESE LESSONS BE APPLIED ELSEWHERE?

We have been describing a project which ran for five years in Nottingham. Inevitably we have at times slipped over from description into abstract recommendations for schemes of this type, but how far can our experience be applied to other places? Obviously, we cannot think in terms of a blue-print when one of our main emphases has been on moulding the service to the locality, and any attempt at similar work would have to take into account such factors as the size of the area, the strength of neighbourhood feeling and the nature and attitudes of existing local authority services. Nevertheless, we feel that the flexibility of this approach should make it possible for similar experiments to be tried elsewhere, and to benefit from the strengths and advantages which we have described.

To be effective, however, the work will need to be taken seriously, and almost certainly require full-time staff. All the indications appear to be that there will in future be an increasing number of professional community workers, and to involve them in schemes of this nature could be to bring valuable insights and open up new sources of recruitment for the old people's welfare field. It could also be a solution to some of the present difficulties of a lack of career structure for old people's welfare workers if there was to be more interchange of staff with other branches of social services.

The working situation is important and, as we have indicated above, there were real advantages in the close link between the OPWC and the CSS. It would be very interesting to see whether the same advantages would be possible within a local authority social services department. Wherever the

* For an explanation of this term, see Chapter 8, page 76.

worker is situated, he will need adequate support, both from fellow professionals and in terms of administrative backing. Like any other form of social service, community work will not be enhanced by being forced to survive on a shoe-string.

We have shown how community development techniques can be applied in one social work situation, that of old people's welfare. In so doing we have worked on the assumption that community development is a *technique* of social intervention, rather than a particular professional job. If this is valid, then it is worth raising the question of whether similar techniques cannot be used in other welfare spheres (and indeed in fields far removed from welfare, such as adult education or town planning).

Bearing in mind the emphasis in the Seebohm Report on area social work teams responding to local community needs,* it may be that some of our findings could have a very wide application.

Inevitably, in thinking of the applicability of the lessons learned in this project, we have concentrated on the employment of professionals. It would be wrong, however, if we did not close by paying tribute to those whose work was the essence of the scheme: the members of care groups, the school pupils, church and community association members and good neighbours who have cared for their elderly fellow-citizens and in so doing have enhanced the quality of life in their city. It was this, not refining professional techniques, which was the object of the project.

* *Report of the Committee on Local Authority and Allied Personal Social Services* (Cmnd. 3703; London, HMSO, 1968), paras. 501–7.

PART III

Wider Issues

CHAPTER 8

The Community

We have kept referring to 'the community' but what exactly do we mean by it? There is a great danger of being mesmerised by the term, until one begins to imagine that there is an actual entity which does things—holds opinions, cares for people, fights local bureaucracy or whatever. This is, of course, nonsense. Communities do not take action: people do. A community is the sum of all the personal networks of reciprocal relationships that exist between people in an area. In the context of community care, the Seebohm Report provides a useful description:

'The term "community" is usually understood to cover both the physical location and the common identity of a group of people. The definition of a community, however, or even of a neighbourhood, is increasingly difficult as society becomes more mobile and people belong to "communities" of common interest, influenced by their work, education, or social activities, as well as where they live. Thus, although traditionally the idea of a community has rested upon geographical locality, and this remains an important aspect of many communities, today different members of a family may belong to different communities of interest as well as the same local neighbourhood. The notion of a community implies the existence of a network of reciprocal social relationships, which among other things ensure mutual aid and give those who experience it a sense of well-being.'*

THE CARING COMMUNITY

This caring takes place within a social situation and involves a wide range of individuals and institutions, both formal and informal. To quote the Seebohm Report again, this time on the subject of mental health:

'The employment and resettlement services of the Department of Employment and Productivity, the Supplementary Benefits Commission, local education and housing departments, home helps and home nurses, probation

* *Report of the Committee on Local Authority and Allied Personal Social Services* (Cmnd. 3703; London, HMSO, 1968), para. 476.

and after-care, the police, the churches, voluntary societies and, most important, employers, workmates, friends, neighbours and landlords, as well as the local authority mental health services all play their part. This is what is meant by the community caring.'*

It is useful to consider the variety of 'carers' who are listed here. We can identify two groups. On the one hand there are the formal social services, and on the other are many other groups with whom the individual in need will have contact in the course of his day-to-day life—his family, his neighbours, those with whom he works, and other organisations, such as churches or community associations which may regard caring for others as, so to speak, a by-product of their other activities. If we are to think about 'the caring community' then it is groups like this that we must consider.

The family

The family, of course, remains the main focus within which people meet and solve their problems, and this is as true for the elderly as for anyone else. While not a panacea for every need, the family is likely to be of prime importance in countering isolation and loneliness, and in providing care and help in the home for old people who are frail or sick. It may also be able to obviate, or at any rate lessen, some of the other problems of old age, such as housing or finance. Unfortunately, despite the very considerable support which old people continue to receive from their families,† there are still large numbers for whom such help is limited or non-existent. Increased geographical mobility, even within the boundaries of a city, may separate families; the design of much modern housing precludes the possibility of three-generation households; while social and demographic changes mean that, compared with fifty years ago, many elderly people have no relatives, or have to rely for help on only one or two children: the demands on a relatively small number of people thus become greater, especially since more old people are living to an advanced age as a result of increases in medical knowledge. In a society in which great emphasis is placed on the needs and importance of young children, one can imagine real conflicts being created for young families faced with the responsibility of caring for elderly parents as well.

* *Report of the Committee on Local Authority and Allied Personal Social Services* (Cmnd. 3703; London, HMSO, 1968), para. 337.

† For a statistical analysis of some of this very considerable support (e.g. 42% of elderly people with children live with them) see Shanas, E., and others, *Old People in Three Industrial Societies* (London, Routledge and Kegan Paul, 1968), chapters 6–7.

Neighbours

Much of the support which the elderly receive from their families may also be available, in a more attenuated form, from nearby neighbours—companionship, care in illness or practical assistance (shopping, gardening, decorating, etc.). Obviously there will be limiting factors which would not apply to the family: neighbours are not likely to feel the same kind of responsibilities that families acknowledge towards their elderly dependents, nor, in view of other commitments, are they likely to give so much help. Nevertheless, their assistance is likely to be motivated by locally-accepted standards of 'neighbourliness' rather than by that self-conscious altruism which we call 'voluntary service'. In simpler terms, they are nice to people because they take it for granted that this is the way in which good neighbours behave to one another. It carries with it, in consequence, some attitude of reciprocal help, which may make it easier both to give and to accept help.

A further perspective of neighbourhood help may be that given by local shopkeepers and tradesmen. We have described how one care group benefited from involving the local sub-postmaster, who cashed most of the pensions in the area concerned, and was ideally placed to act as an 'early-warning' device. Other tradesmen, especially corner shopkeepers who serve a small area and know their customers well, and those who visit people in their own homes—postmen, milkmen, window cleaners, insurance agents, etc.—can all help, especially in notifying the appropriate services in the event of an old person's being ill. Attempts to create links at city level between the OPWC and home delivery services were not very successful, but some care groups managed to establish useful contacts among them. Individual instances are also recorded of postmen who lit the fire for old people in the morning, and of an insurance agent who helped some of his elderly customers in a number of ways, including cutting their toe-nails.

In discussing the attitudes of families and neighbours we do not want to imply any moral judgement about the desirability of these arrangements. We simply want to make the point that in various groups within society, attitudes of this kind may be accepted as normal, and that agreement about such responsibilities may be greater than is sometimes realised. Reliance on such 'natural' forms of help may be limited, however. On the one hand we must allow for old people who wish to maintain their independence from their families—to keep their own homes, to deal with their needs in their own way, rather than becoming dependent on their children. On the other hand, it would be wrong to see the social services simply as a substitute for family or neighbourhood support. Very often they are that, of course, but they may also meet needs which the best organised family cannot tackle from within its own resources. The most obvious example of this is specialised medical care, but one could also instance the need for skilled assistance and advice in the field of mental health; or, to take a completely different perspective, the provision of old people's clubs through which the elderly can, by voluntary and conscious choice, meet their recreational needs in the company of their contemporaries. This distinction between services which are a substitute for family and neighbourhood support and those which supplement such support with specialist provision, is of crucial importance in old people's welfare policy.*

Secondary volunteers

Turning to the welfare role of institutions in the community, a distinction can be made between formal social services and other associations of which caring activities are a by-product of their major functions, and whose members we have therefore described as 'secondary volunteers'. These bodies may include churches, schools, community and tenants' associations, social and recreational clubs, trade unions and staff associations and the police force. While care groups did not establish links with all these bodies it will be clear from Tables 1 and 4 that some of them, particularly churches and community associations, had a crucial role in the formation and maintenance of the majority of care groups. Leaders and employees of these organisations—clergy, teachers, wardens of community centres—tend to be regarded as having leadership roles within the local community, and to be approached with a variety of requests for help from the people of the neighbourhood. They thus form nodal points in a local care system and are often anxious in consequence to find resources to meet the needs which are brought to them. At the same time they are often able to provide organisational expertise in the early stages of development of care schemes.

A second and equally obvious point about these organisations is the potential resources which they can mobilise from among their membership, though against this must be set the calls on their time to keep their own organisations running.

In introducing the concept of resources our perspective starts to shift. When we discuss families and neighbours, we are basically concerned with identifying what may already exist in the community, and framing caring policies to take into account and support such activities. Once we move on to consider formal associations which have taken some conscious decision to

* This distinction is made by Peter Townsend: see Townsend, P. and Wedderburn, D. C.: *The Aged in the Welfare State* (London, Bell, 1965), chapter 2.

aid the elderly, we can start thinking in terms of deployment of resources, so as to ensure their optimum use. In terms of social work activity, we have moved from support of the individual and his family to the fields of community development and, particularly, community organisation. This becomes more apparent when we start identifying the more formal social services, including groups of 'primary' volunteers whose main purpose in coming together is to undertake some form of service. We have already seen that one of the aims of care groups from their inception was to co-ordinate services for the elderly in the care group's area, and this has clearly continued to be an important part in their role.

'Volunteer'—role or function?

We tend to think of the volunteer as someone with a particular role, whose capabilities and needs must be carefully considered. What has been argued above, however, is that there are vast numbers of people in the community who fulfil exactly the same function as the volunteer, but who are not formally identified as 'volunteers': instead their role is that of relation, neighbour, shopkeeper, milkman, church member or whatever. If the main concern is that elderly people should be cared for when they need it, it follows that we should try to identify all the means by which this is achieved, not just those to which we can attach the label 'social service'. Consequently a scheme for community care can be seen to have within its purview the whole community, and the quality of life of the people who make up that community. It becomes, in this way, at once a wider and more sophisticated and delicate approach. It involves on the one hand working with what is there—mobilising, harnessing and strengthening the resources that already exist in the community and which help far more people than we can ever hope to assist with our puny social services. But on the other hand, if we are to involve the community, if we are to try to develop its resources, then we must be aware of what we are doing, and of its total ramifications in all the different fields that affect people's lives; social, economic and political. We are just beginning to wake up to the fact that if we tinker with out natural environment we may create results reaching far beyond what we intended: we should be equally aware of the impact of social change, whether intended or not, on our social environment.

Who cares?

The formal volunteer is at a disadvantage compared to the neighbour or the family: he is 'doing good'. The term 'do-gooder' has had an unfortunate and an unfair history, but its overtones may reflect a real difficulty. There are likely to be differences in the relationship between volunteers and an old person and that between the same old person and her family or neighbours. In the latter case there is a 'natural' relationship based on commonly-accepted patterns of behaviour that carry with them implications of reciprocity and a recognition that both sides have obligations as well as rights. In the former case, all the giving is on one side, all the receiving on the other, and this can carry with it implications of dependency that may reinforce the old person's concept of himself as a useless and helpless member of society. The phrase 'poor old souls' is heard in old people's welfare circles just that little bit too often for comfort.

Of course, many old people may never experience these feelings, and for others the formal implications of the difference in role may quickly evaporate as a friendship with the volunteer develops. But we should be aware of the possible implications for community care. If people think that there is a difference in status between givers and receivers it may influence their willingness to adopt either role, particularly if these differences in *dependency* status are also interpreted by those concerned as differences in *social* status. Although it is far from being the whole truth, we know that many formal volunteers come, for a variety of reasons, from the middle class. If 'volunteering' is interpreted by potential volunteers as a middle-class activity—and still more if the recipients of their efforts are thought to be predominantly working-class—then these attitudes could be reflected in an unwillingness of working-class people to appear better than their neighbours by becoming formal volunteers, and an unwillingness among middle-class people to seem to lose status by becoming recipients of voluntary help.

It is important not to over-emphasise this aspect of voluntary care: as we have indicated already, the idea almost certainly will not occur to people in many situations, and the work in Nottingham could show many working-class volunteers and middle-class recipients. Nevertheless, it could be used as a partial explanation of the failure or sluggishness of some schemes in the middle-class areas, and point to the importance of emphasising 'neighbourliness' rather than 'volunteering' in some working-class districts. It is perhaps a tenable suggestion that there may be problems in the recruitment and use of volunteers in areas where there is a strong homogeneity of class, because of the failure of most forms of voluntary service to provide any possibility of reciprocal action by the recipient.

THE REPRESENTATIVE COMMUNITY

One consequence of thinking of the community as a distinct entity which has needs, cares for its members and the rest of it, may be to assume that 'the community' can express itself through a single mouthpiece. If, for example, a local planning authority is told that it must consult the local community about its proposals, and finds a local body calling itself a community council or some such title, then both sides may come to believe that by discussions between the two 'the community' has been consulted. But has it? Obviously, we cannot tell until we know how representative the community group is, but at first sight it would be surprising if a body with say, a mailing list of 200 and an active membership of fifty should be adequately representative of the views and wishes of an area containing perhaps 20,000 people, many of whose wishes may be mutually contradictory at a quite basic level.

How representative are community groups? How representative can they be, and how can they be representative? And does it matter? Perhaps we can start by considering what we mean by 'representative'. At one level it may simply mean that the attitudes of a given group are similar to those of a larger body. This is the assumption made in opinion polls and research exercises—that the answers received from one randomly selected group of people are likely to be similar to the answers of any other group selected by the same method. In this context, for a community group to be representative it may require little more than that the members of the group are local residents or in some other way members of the community (although they are very unlikely to be as typical or 'representative' as a random sample would be) and the planning department in our example might ask them for their opinions just as it might ask the local Mothers' Union or the queue at the supermarket.

But things change as soon as it is claimed that the community group has some special additional right to be consulted, and that its views should carry particular weight with the local authority. At this stage other people both locally and at city level may start to ask 'Why your views rather than ours? What right have you got to speak for the whole community?' It is the answer to this question, the justification for a community group's claim to be representative, that we have referred to in earlier sections of this report at 'legitimacy'.

Legitimacy

Claims for legitimacy can be based on various types of evidence, which we might term the administrative, expertise, and local credibility arguments. Administratively, members of a group may be able to point out that it is deliberately structured to involve as many interests and individuals as possible, that when it was set up efforts were made to inform and involve everyone in the area, that frequent and well-publicised meetings are held, that the committee includes representatives from sub-areas or different interest groups and so on. These and similar techniques may be used to try to ensure that the group is as representative and as open as possible, thereby at least providing a negative justification for the group—that anyone who wishes to participate can be involved and is encouraged to do so.

Secondly, a group may claim legitimacy because of expert knowledge. This can either be the experience of living in a situation—'only those who live in high blocks of flats know what it's like'—or because through offering a service a group becomes aware of the problems of local people. Obviously, groups might claim more expertise in some areas of concern than in others—a care group might claim to be very knowledgeable about the needs of old people in its area, but know much less about, say, employment opportunities for school leavers. With this kind of claim, justification must depend in the last resort on the amount of hard evidence in terms of numbers of individual cases that the group can produce.

The third and most important type of legitimacy, though also the most difficult to demonstrate, is simply whether or not the group is accepted by local people as a forum where their needs can be expressed, and as a spokesman to represent these views to the authorities. Short of asking everyone in the area for their views there are few ways of determining this, but the steady expansion of neighbourhood groups and the increased participation of local people in their activities may be taken as an indication of a growing interest in community groups. If we can also find evidence of trust in their work then legitimacy is reasonably ensured.

Of course, for many activities the question of legitimacy will not be very important, and it may be felt that in this discussion we have come a long way from neighbourhood care for the elderly, but even in this field at some stage a care group will want to demand more services for the elderly and will then have to justify its claim. Still more, those groups which become involved in other, more contentious fields such as town planning will be called on to indicate the extent to which they are representative of their neighbourhood. They may have a very sound reply, but they will need to be aware of the grounds on which they make it, and to recognise the great variety of individuals and groups which make up a community.

Finally, we return to the point from which we started. Communities are not single monolithic entities: they contain a plurality of interests, just as the wider society does, and however representative a community group may be, it is unlikely that it will be able to contain all these different views. The representative nature of community groups is important, but they need to recognise their limitations, and must not expect to establish a monopoly as the voice of the community.

COMMUNITY CARE AND SOCIAL POLICY

We began by describing how Nottingham responded to certain national and local trends; we end by suggesting some implications of Nottingham's experience which might be applied, if not nationally, then at least in a wide number of situations.

Community work and community care

The basic aim of the project was to discover whether it was possible to foster and support local community initiatives in caring for the elderly, using community development methods. This was undertaken with two background assumptions in mind:

1 that to be fully effective a service must be responsive to the individual and that this means helping him in his own situation locally;
2 that the local community contained resources for helping people which could only be tapped at local level.

We believe that the project described in this report bears out these assumptions, and that in particular techniques of community development are as relevant to community care as they are to other types of community work. These techniques carry with them certain implications—on the one hand what might be described as a sociological approach to welfare, taking into account the local social structure, attitudes and resources rather than adopting a blanket policy approach, and on the other hand a non-directive approach to community groups which allows people to determine their own objectives and means of achieving them.

This approach may at times produce a dilemma for the worker and for his agency: is his primary loyalty to old people, or to the community group with which he is working? We should emphasise that this problem did not arise in Nottingham but one could envisage a situation in which, for example, a community group devoted all its attention to a proposed road-building programme, and ignored the clamant needs of elderly people in the area. It could be argued that this is only a microcosmic illustration of the way in which all social workers are limited by the willingness of the public to make resources available, whether these resources are voluntary service or finance supplied through rates and taxes, but the dilemma still exists for the agency, and it is partly for this reason that we see advantages of work of this kind being based in an agency concerned with diverse forms of community work.

What the community offers

The key point about this approach to community care is to seize on what the community can offer, and this is a great deal. There is plenty of evidence that, far from having left everything to the welfare state, vast numbers of people care for their relatives, their neighbours, and other people in their locality. Local people can provide immediate help, continuous service, companionship and, for want of a better term, keeping an eye on things, in a way that the official services can never hope to match. They can also, because they are so so close to the situation, provide feed-back about people's real needs which is essential if services are to be effective.

What the community needs

If the community is to fulfil this role, however, it needs support. Individuals need help or advice from trained social workers when a situation is too much for them to manage alone. Community groups need advice, stimulation, encouragement; they also need straightforward administrative and financial help at times. All these may be made more possible as local authority social service departments decentralise their activities to area offices, and the social workers, for their part, will find many allies, as well as invaluable two-way channels of communication.

It should be stressed that a policy of neighbourhood involvement in community care will not provide services on the cheap. It will bring to light many needs of which the social services were not previously aware; it will make more demands both on specialised services such as mental health and on the regular domiciliary services such as home helps, and it will involve social workers in attending meetings of care groups and supporting their members. The social services and the local community are not substitutes for one another; they are both indispensable parts of a humane provision for those members of our society who need help.

Appendices

APPENDIX I

Definitions

Community organisation (or, more accurately, community *welfare* organisation) has been defined as 'the process of bringing about and maintaining adjustment between social welfare needs and social welfare resources in a geographical area or a special field of service'.* In other words it means identifying people's needs and then trying to ensure that the right services are provided in the most appropriate way to meet those needs. It thus involves both the co-ordination of services and the establishment of links between the services and those who receive them, in order to ensure that the service provided is what people actually want. This has for a long time been the role of councils of social service and, in respect of specific groups in need, of such bodies as old people's welfare councils.

Community development involves some of the same ideas, since it is also concerned with ensuring that people get what they want, but here the emphasis is on enabling them first to identify what they require, and then to obtain it. The definition that follows was framed to describe the use of community development techniques in developing countries, but it is also relevant for industrial, urban societies:

> 'Community development . . . [is] the process by which the efforts of the people themselves are united with those of governmental authorities to improve the economic, social and cultural conditions of communities, to integrate these communities into the life of the nation and to enable them to contribute fully to national progress.
>
> This complex of processes is then made up of two essential elements: the participation of the people themselves in efforts to improve their level of living with as much reliance as possible on their own initiative; and the provision of technical and other services in ways which encourage initiative, self-help and mutual aid and make these more effective. It is expressed in programmes to achieve a wide variety of specific improvements.'†

It will be seen from this that community development can cover a much wider area than social welfare, and as we have seen community groups in Nottingham involved themselves in a wide variety of activities. Community development is a self-help exercise: it gets people to define their needs and then says: 'O.K., what are you going to do about it?' It also commonly involves some professional support, and at times even initiative in the first instance, from outside the area. Community development workers

* Dunham, A., *Community Welfare Organisation: Principles and Practice*; New York, Thomas Y. Crowell Co., 1958, p. 23.

† Report of a *European Seminar on Training for Community Development*; U.N., Geneva, 1962, p. 8.

who give this support have been variously described as 'enablers', 'encouragers' and 'catalysts' who help to transmute vague aspirations into positive actions. They also play an important role as links between the local neighbourhood and the wider community, particularly in helping to secure resources—of money, services and expertise—for local projects.

A third aspect of community work, which is growing in importance, though there have so far been few attempts at definition, is *community action*. This is generally applied to some form of militant action directed at securing resources for a neighbourhood or group of people. It might include, for example, a group of mothers blocking a road in order to demand a pedestrian crossing for their children, or council tenants staging a rent strike to try to compel the corporation to carry out repairs to their property. It may thus appear rather different from the self-help philosophy of community development, but in fact it may be a relevant response to the needs of an area: in modern society many needs can only be met by specialist services or resources controlled by those in authority. Community action may thus be a strategy within the framework of community development (and vice versa), but it may also be used by people who reject the community development approach as being too much aligned with the power structure, and who would want to take a more revolutionary view of society.

Community work is often used as an umbrella description for any variety of these and similar forms of activity.

APPENDIX 2

Statistics broken down by care groups

TABLE A1

Source of first approach or initiative in the establishment of care schemes

	Church	*School*	*Community association*	*Residents' association*	*Councillor*	*Hospital*	*Over-60 club*	*Individual volunteer*	*Individual in need*
Aspley	x				x				
Bestwood	x								
Bilborough and Beechdale	x	x							
Broxtowe	x		x						
Clifton	x								
Lenton Abbey	x								
Lenton and Dunkirk	x						x		
Meadows									
Radford					x				
Sherwood						x			
Sneinton								x	
St Ann's				x					
Wollaton	x								
Wollaton Park									x

TABLE A2

Communication systems between care groups and old people

	Door to door survey	*Pre-paid card*	*Postcard*	*Posters*	*Neighbours*	*Street warden*	*Care group worker*	*Organisations, Health and Welfare Department*	*Circular*
Aspley	x					x			
Bestwood	x							x	
Bilborough and Beechdale	x			x				x	x
Broxtowe	x								
Clifton	x		x	x				x	
Lenton Abbey									x
Lenton and Dunkirk				x				x	x
Meadows	x	x		x	x		x	x	
Radford		x		x				x	
Sherwood		x		x				x	
Sneinton				x					x
St Ann's					x		x	x	
Wollaton						x			x
Wollaton Park			x	x				x	x

TABLE A3

Services developed by care groups

	Lunch club	*Day centre*	*Meals on wheels*	*Garden-ing, decorat-ing, etc.*	*Shop-ping and library*	*Visiting*	*Christ-mas parcels*	*Started clubs*	*Visit-ing hospitals*	*Move-ment to music*	*Post-hospital care*	*Meals week-ends*
Aspley				x		x						
Bestwood	x			x	x	x	x					
Bilborough				x	x	x						
Broxtowe	x			x		x						
Clifton			x	x		x	x	x	x		x	
Lenton Abbey				x	x	x						
Lenton and Dunkirk				x	x	x	x				x	
Meadows	x	x		x	x	x	x	x		x	x	x
Radford	x				x	x			x		x	
Sherwood	x			x	x	x	x				x	x
Sneinton						x						
St Ann's	x											
Wollaton				x		x						
Wollaton Park				x	x	x	x	x	x	x	x	

TABLE A4

Involvement of statutory workers with care groups

	Welfare department	*Mental welfare*	*Home help*	*Children's department*	*Medical social workers*	*District nurse*	*Health visitor*	*Department of Health and Social Security*	*General practitioners*	*Probation department*
Aspley	AR		R	A				A		R
Bestwood	AR	R		A		AR	AR			
Bilborough					R					
Broxtowe	R			A						A
Clifton	APR	R	R		R	R	R		R	
Lenton Abbey	AR					AR				
Lenton and Dunkirk	AR				R	R				
Meadows	APR	AR	AR	A	R	AR	AR	A	R	A
Radford	AR				R	R			R	
Sherwood	AR	AR			R	AR	AR			
Sneinton	AR									
St Ann's	AR									
Wollaton										
Wollaton Park	AR				R				R	

Key: A = attended meetings, P = involved in project, R = referred cases

TABLE A5

Involvement of voluntary bodies with care groups

	Churches	*Youth groups*	*School social service groups*	*Over-sixty clubs*	*Community associations*	*Tenants' or residents' associations*	*NOPWC*	*Red Cross*	*University or college of education*	*Guild for the disabled*	*WRVS*
Aspley	APR						APR				
Bestwood	APR	P	A	AR		A	APR				
Bilborough	AR	AP	PR	A	AR		APR				
Broxtowe	APR		P	AP	APR		APR				P
Clifton	APR	AP	AP	A	APR		APR		AP	R	
Lenton Abbey	AR			A			APR		AP		
Lenton and Dunkirk	AR	AP	P	AP	APR	APR	APR		AP		P
Meadows	APR	AP	PR	A	APR		APR	R	AP	R	P
Radford	R	AP	P	A		R	APR		P		P
Sherwood	APR	P	P	A	APR	AR	APR	R	P		
Sneinton	AR		PR	A			APR				
St Ann's	APR	P				APR	APR		P		P
Wollaton	AR						APR				
Wollaton Park	AR		AP	A	A		APR				

Key: A = attended meetings, P = involved in project, R = referred cases

TABLE A6

Officers of care groups by background at time of first establishment of group

	Clergymen		*Local residents*			*Non-local volunteer*	
	C	S	C	S	T	C	S
Aspley			x	x			
Bestwood	x	x					
Bilborough and Beechdale	x			x			
Broxtowe		x	x				
Clifton	x			x			
Lenton Abbey	x			x			
Lenton and Dunkirk			x	x	x		
Meadows	x						x
Radford				x		x	
Sherwood	x			x			
Sneinton			x	x	x		
St Ann's				x	x	x	
Wollaton	x	x					
Wollaton Park	x			x			
	8	3	4	10	3	2	1

Key: C = chairman, S = secretary, T = treasurer

TABLE A7

Location of administrative bases

	Church			*Community association*			*Home*			*Other (e.g. shop)*		
	FP	CM	ADM	FP	CM	ADM	FP	CM	ADM	FP	CM	ADM
Aspley		x					x		x			
Bestwood	x	x	x									
Bilborough and Beechdale										x		
Broxtowe	x		x		x	x						
Clifton		x			x		x		x			
Lenton Abbey	x	x					x		x			
Lenton and Dunkirk					x		x		x			
Meadows	x			x	x	x						
Radford		x					x		x			
Sherwood				x	x	x	x		x			
Sneinton		x					x		x			
St Ann's		x							x	x	x	x
Wollaton	x	x	x									
Wollaton Park		x					x		x	x		

Key: FP = focal point, CM = committee meetings, ADM = administration

TABLE A8

Finance of care groups

	Local authority		*Trust*		*OPWC*		*Rotary, etc.*		*Own fundraising*			
	A	S	A	S	A	S	A	S	*Social*	*Jumble sale*	*Prize draw*	*Collect-ing tin*
Aspley									x	x		
Bestwood		x			x			x				
Bilborough and Beechdale												
Broxtowe					x				x			
Clifton	x	x			x			x	x		x	x
Lenton Abbey					x							
Lenton and Dunkirk					x				x			x
Meadows	x	x	x		x			x	x	x	x	x
Radford					x					x		
Sherwood	x	x							x	x		x
Sneinton					x							
St Ann's			x				x		x	x	x	
Wollaton												
Wollaton Park					x				x			

Key: A = administration, S = service

APPENDIX 3

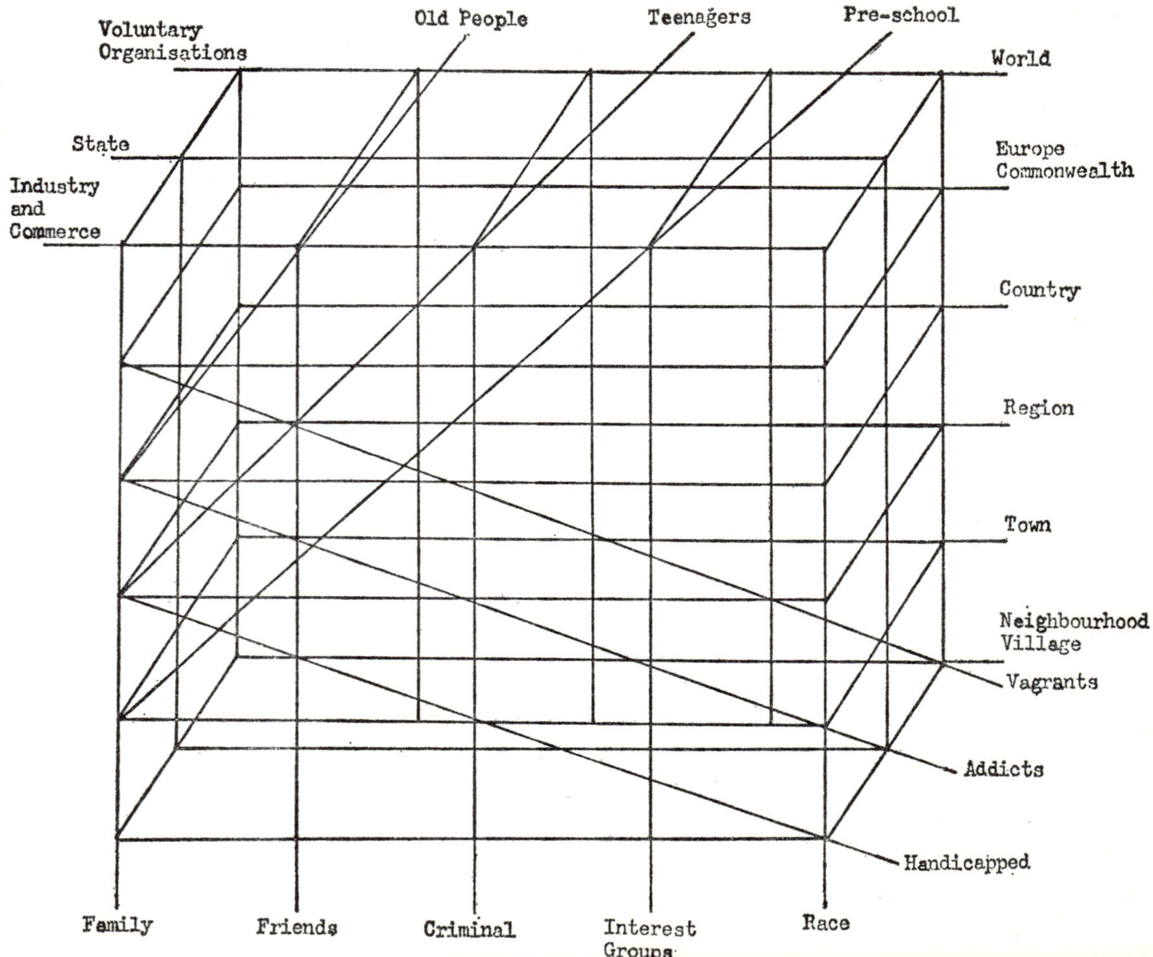
Voluntary Organisations
Old People
Teenagers
Pre-school
World
State
Industry and Commerce
Europe Commonwealth
Country
Region
Town
Neighbourhood Village
Vagrants
Addicts
Handicapped
Family
Friends
Criminal
Interest Groups
Race

Note on the crate concept of community:

The diagram shows at its very simplest a concept of society which suggests that individuals may be connected with innumerable networks which he influences and which influence him.

The individual is seen as belonging to a geographical dimension shown as horizontal layers within which he may belong to one or several social groupings—shown on the vertical dimensions extending across geographical boundaries.

Cutting through the geographical and social groupings are large institutions such as machinery of 'state'.

Society identifies particular 'age groups' and 'needs groups' as shown in the diagonal lines.

The extent to which a community worker can identify these networks and assess their influence will have far-reaching implications for his ability to be effective in his work.